Christmas Cottage
COOKBOOK

Christmas Cottage
COOKBOOK

VOLUME 1~DECORATIONS, RECIPES & GIFTS FOR THE HOLIDAYS

FROM THE PUBLISHERS OF

hm|books

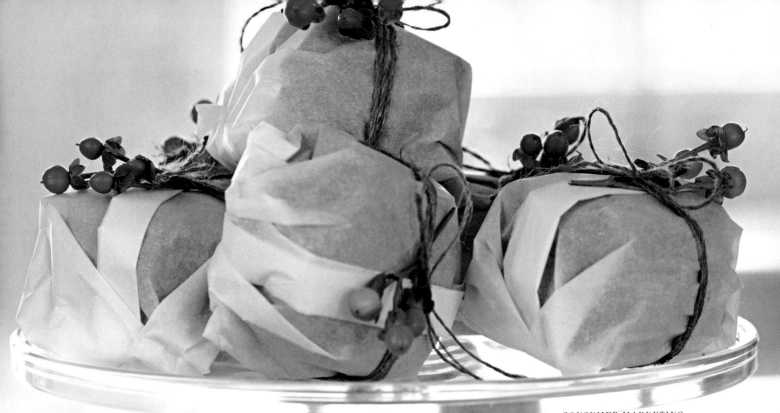

hm | books

EXECUTIVE VICE PRESIDENT/CCO Brian K. Hoffman

VICE PRESIDENT/EDITORIAL Cindy Smith Cooper

ART DIRECTOR Tracy Wood-Franklin

COTTAGE JOURNAL EDITORIAL

EDITOR-IN-CHIEF Phyllis Hoffman DePiano
EDITORIAL DIRECTOR Cindy Smith Cooper
EDITOR Linda Baltzell Wright
CREATIVE DIRECTOR/PHOTOGRAPHY Mac Jamieson
ART DIRECTOR Karissa Brown
ILLUSTRATOR Marie Barber
CONTRIBUTING WRITERS Angie Brown, Tanya L. Cooper,
Lauren Eberle, May Knowlton, Lorna Reeves
COPY EDITORS Nancy Meeks, Nancy Ogburn, Terri Robertson
CONTRIBUTING COPY EDITOR Donna Baldone
CONTRIBUTING STYLISTS Adrienne Allredge Williams,
Renee Beaty, Lucy Finney, Yukie McLean
SENIOR PHOTOGRAPHERS John O'Hagan, Marcy Black Simpson
PHOTOGRAPHERS William Dickey, Stephanie Welbourne Grund,
Sarah Swihart, Kamin Williams
CONTRIBUTING PHOTOGRAPHERS Tanya L. Cooper,
Kimberly Finkel Davis, Tria Giovan
TEST KITCHEN DIRECTOR Janice Ritter
EXECUTIVE CHEF Rebecca Treadwell
TEST KITCHEN PROFESSIONALS Virginia Hornbuckle,
Kathleen Kanen, Janet Lambert, Aimee Bishop Lindsey,
Elizabeth Nelson, Loren Wood
TEST KITCHEN ASSISTANT Anita Simpson Spain
CONTRIBUTING TEST KITCHEN PROFESSIONAL Jane Drennen
SENIOR DIGITAL IMAGING SPECIALIST Delisa McDaniel
DIGITAL IMAGING SPECIALIST Clark Densmore
WEB DEVELOPER John-Mark Taylor
WEB DESIGNER Glenda Cunningham
SPECIAL PROJECTS DIRECTOR Brenda McClain

CONSUMER MARKETING

CONSUMER MARKETING DIRECTOR Tricia Wagner
ONLINE MARKETING DIRECTOR Missy Polhemus
CONSUMER MARKETING MANAGER Allison Mills Greenhalgh
CONSUMER MARKETING DESIGNER Julie Haggard

ADMINISTRATIVE

IT DIRECTOR Matthew Scott Holt
HUMAN RESOURCES DIRECTOR Judy Brown Lazenby
ADMINISTRATIVE DIRECTOR Lynn Lee Terry

hm
hoffmanmedia

PRESIDENT Phyllis Hoffman DePiano
EXECUTIVE VICE PRESIDENT/COO Eric W. Hoffman
EXECUTIVE VICE PRESIDENT/CCO Brian K. Hoffman
EXECUTIVE VICE PRESIDENT/CFO G. Marc Neas
VICE PRESIDENT/MANUFACTURING Greg Baugh
VICE PRESIDENT/EDITORIAL Cindy Smith Cooper
VICE PRESIDENT/CONSUMER MARKETING Silvia Rider

Hoffman Media
1900 International Park Drive, Suite 50
Birmingham, Alabama 35243
www.hoffmanmedia.com

ISBN # 978-0-9770069-1-5
Printed in Mexico

On the cover: Spice Cake with Fluffy
White Frosting, page 200
Photography by Marcy Simpson
Styling by Yukie McLean
Food styling by Kathleen Kanen

116

223

Contents

INTRODUCTION

There's no doubt that it's the most wonderful time of the year. And yet, in the hustle and bustle of the holiday season, it's easy to lose your holly-jolly spirit. That's why we're delighted to offer you *Christmas Cottage Cookbook*, packed with delicious recipes, festive décor, and great gift ideas sure to inspire you to create the cozy Christmas you've dreamed about.

Relax in knowing that our pages are filled with creative inspiration to make your season a cinch. In these next few months of planning and preparation, let us be your keepsake companion as you deck the halls and design your menus. You might keep a scrapbook of your own ideas, too, gathering snapshots from Christmases past to complement fresh new tips full of cheer.

When it comes to perfecting your Christmas style, remember that cherished collections and antiques can play an important part. Home is the place where we proudly display our precious and prized treasures passed from generation to generation. Even our beloved trees can become a showcase of special gifts as tiny handmade mementos of childhood take a prominent position on the elegant evergreen.

Of course, gathering around the table is what holiday memories are truly made of. We hold hands and say grace as we delight in decadent meals made by those we love. The familiar yet delicious tom turkey or fancy beef tenderloin anchors a delightful array of vegetable side dishes and salads. Desserts of sweet pies and cakes are the crowning touch—whether just a bite or a whole slice, these tempting treats are best served with a warm beverage and laughter by the fire.

Most of all, it's our Christmas wish that your season of celebration be filled with family and friends, with comfort and joy. Because it's when we show a welcoming spirit through open doors and open hearts that our cozy cottages feel the most like home.

May your days be merry and bright, *Cindy*

Holiday Menus of
PLENTY

Gathering around the table with cherished family and friends for a sumptuous feast goes hand in hand with the holidays. Whether enjoying plentiful pancakes or traditional turkey, partaking in delightful meals together makes each moment— and Christmas memory—extra special.

CRANBERRY-CIDER FIZZ

Cheery and Bright

DECK THE TABLE WITH MINIATURE TREES AND REINDEER
AS WELL AS LIVELY LINENS FOR A MAGICAL CHRISTMAS
MORNING WITH THE FAMILY. A STACK OF OUR WILD
BLUEBERRY-SOUR CREAM PANCAKES DRIZZLED WITH
SWEET SYRUP IS A DELICIOUS WAY TO WAKE UP.

On the Menu

Ham Steaks with Maple and Mustard   Parmesan-baked Eggs
Potato Casserole with Smoked Salmon and Horseradish Cream
Wild Blueberry-Sour Cream Pancakes with Walnut-Spice Butter
Caramel-glazed Cranberry Bundt Cake
Strawberry-Kiwifruit Salad   Cranberry-Cider Fizz

Ham Steaks with Maple and Mustard

Makes about 12 servings

2 tablespoons canola oil, divided
3 bone-in ham steaks (about
   1 pound each), divided
¼ cup firmly packed dark brown sugar
¼ cup pure maple syrup
2 tablespoons spicy brown mustard

1. Preheat oven to 350°. In a large skillet, heat 2 teaspoons oil over medium-high heat. Pat 1 ham steak dry with a paper towel. Place ham in skillet; cook 2 minutes per side or until lightly browned. Place ham on a large rimmed baking sheet. Repeat procedure twice with remaining oil and ham.

2. In a small saucepan, combine brown sugar, syrup, and mustard. Bring to a simmer over medium heat, stirring occasionally. Reduce heat to low; simmer 2 minutes. Spread 3 tablespoons maple syrup mixture over ham. Cover and set aside remaining maple syrup mixture. Bake ham steaks, uncovered, for 10 minutes.

3. Cut ham into serving pieces; place on a platter. Drizzle with remaining maple syrup mixture.

Wild Blueberry-Sour Cream Pancakes with Walnut-Spice Butter

Makes about 24 (4-inch) pancakes

3¾ cups self-rising flour
⅔ cup sugar
½ teaspoon salt
1½ cups milk
1½ cups sour cream
6 tablespoons vegetable oil
3 large eggs, lightly beaten
1½ teaspoons vanilla extract
1½ cups frozen wild blueberries*,
   unthawed
Walnut-Spice Butter (recipe follows)

1. In a large bowl, combine flour, sugar, and salt. In a medium bowl, whisk together milk, sour cream, oil, eggs, and vanilla. Add milk mixture to flour mixture, stirring just until moistened (batter should be slightly lumpy). Gently fold in blueberries.

2. Heat a lightly greased griddle over medium heat. Pour about ¼ cup batter for each pancake onto hot griddle. Cook until bubbles form on surface of pancakes and edges begin to look dry (about 3 minutes). Turn pancakes over; cook 2 minutes or until done. Serve warm with Walnut-Spice Butter and syrup.

Note: Because frozen blueberries can quickly discolor batter, spoon half of batter into a bowl. Add half of blueberries; cook pancakes as directed. Repeat procedure with remaining batter and blueberries.

*We used Wyman's Frozen Wild Blueberries. These blueberries are small and cook quickly in the batter; no need to thaw.

Walnut-Spice Butter

Makes about 1½ cups

1 cup walnut halves, toasted and
   cooled
1 cup butter, softened
1 teaspoon pumpkin pie spice
¼ cup sugar

1. In the work bowl of a food processor, place walnuts. Pulse 5 times or until coarsely ground.

2. In a medium bowl, place walnuts, butter, and pumpkin pie spice; coarsely mash. On a sheet of wax paper, spoon butter mixture into a 7-inch log. Fold wax paper over butter mixture. Roll up, tightly twisting ends to seal. Refrigerate until firm. Just before serving, sprinkle sugar in a thin layer on a work surface. Unwrap butter; roll in sugar. Cut chilled butter into desired serving sizes.

Parmesan-baked Eggs with Toast Points

Makes 12 servings

9 slices hearty white bread
2 tablespoons butter, melted
3 tablespoons butter, softened
24 large eggs
½ cup heavy whipping cream
½ cup freshly grated Parmesan
  cheese
1 teaspoon salt
1 teaspoon ground black pepper
½ cup chopped seeded tomato
¼ cup finely chopped fresh parsley

1. Preheat oven to 375°. Using a serrated knife, trim crusts from bread; cut each slice of bread into 4 triangles. Place bread on a rimmed baking sheet. Lightly brush both sides of bread with melted butter. Bake for 3 minutes per side or until golden brown.

2. Brush the insides of 12 small shallow gratin dishes or ramekins with softened butter. Crack 2 eggs into one dish, being careful not to break yolks. Drizzle 2 teaspoons cream around egg yolks. Sprinkle with 1 teaspoon cheese. Repeat procedure with remaining eggs, cream, and cheese. Sprinkle with salt and pepper. Place dishes on a large rimmed baking sheet.

3. Bake for about 12 minutes or until eggs are set around edges and slightly jiggly in the center or until desired degree of doneness. Sprinkle with tomato and parsley. Serve with toast.

Strawberry-Kiwifruit Salad
Makes about 12 servings

4 cups halved strawberries
4 cups cubed peeled kiwifruit
½ cup fresh orange juice
2 tablespoons sugar
2 tablespoons honey
½ teaspoon ground cinnamon
½ cup sweetened shredded coconut, toasted
½ cup roasted salted pistachios, chopped
¼ cup pomegranate seeds

1. In a large bowl, combine strawberries and kiwifruit. In a small bowl, whisk together orange juice, sugar, honey, and cinnamon. Pour over fruit; gently toss. Cover and chill at least 1 hour or up to 4 hours. Just before serving, stir in coconut, pistachios, and pomegranate seeds.

Potato Casserole with Smoked Salmon and Horseradish Cream
Makes 12 servings

Horseradish Cream (recipe follows)
2 tablespoons canola oil, divided
2 (28-ounce) bags frozen diced potatoes with onions and peppers, unthawed, divided
8 large eggs
½ cup heavy whipping cream
1½ teaspoons salt
½ cup shredded mozzarella cheese
⅔ cup chopped smoked salmon
1 tablespoon finely chopped fresh chives

1. Prepare Horseradish Cream, and chill.

2. Preheat oven to 350°. Spray bottom and sides of a 13x9-inch baking dish with nonstick cooking spray. In a large nonstick skillet, heat 1 tablespoon oil over medium-high heat. Carefully add 1 bag of potatoes, and cook, stirring occasionally, for 5 to 7 minutes or until lightly browned. Spoon into a large bowl. Repeat procedure with

remaining 1 tablespoon canola oil and remaining 1 bag of potatoes.

3. In a medium bowl, whisk together eggs, cream, and salt. Stir in cheese. Pour egg mixture over potatoes; stir well. Pour potato mixture into prepared baking dish. Bake for 25 to 30 minutes or until set. Let stand 5 minutes before serving. Sprinkle with salmon. Drizzle with ¼ cup Horseradish Cream. Sprinkle with chives. Serve with remaining Horseradish Cream.

Horseradish Cream
Makes about 1¼ cups

1 cup sour cream
½ cup mayonnaise
⅓ cup milk
2 tablespoons prepared horseradish or to taste
½ teaspoon salt

1. In a bowl, combine sour cream, mayonnaise, milk, horseradish, and salt; whisk until smooth. Cover and refrigerate at least 1 hour or up to 2 weeks.

Caramel-glazed Cranberry Bundt Cake
Makes about 12 servings

1 cup dried sweetened cranberries, chopped
½ cup water
1 cup butter, softened
1¾ cups sugar
4 large eggs
2¾ cups self-rising flour
1 cup milk
1 teaspoon orange zest
1 teaspoon vanilla extract
Caramel Glaze (recipe follows)

1. Preheat oven to 350°. Spray a 10- to 15-cup fluted Bundt pan with nonstick baking spray with flour. In a small saucepan, combine cranberries and water. Bring to a boil over medium-high heat; cook 1 minute. Cover and set aside until liquid is absorbed (about 10 minutes). Uncover; cool completely.

2. In a large bowl, combine butter and sugar; beat at medium speed with a mixer until fluffy (about 5 minutes). Add eggs, one at a time, beating well after each addition. Reduce mixer speed to low. Add flour to butter mixture in 3 batches alternately with milk, beginning and ending with flour, stopping to scrape sides of bowl occasionally. Add orange zest and vanilla, beating just until blended. Gently fold in cranberries. Spoon batter into prepared pan. Swirl a knife through batter to break up any air pockets.

3. Bake for 45 minutes or until a wooden pick inserted near the center comes out clean. Cool in pan 10 minutes. Remove from pan, and cool completely on a wire rack. Place cake on a serving plate; drizzle with Caramel Glaze.

Caramel Glaze
Makes about ⅔ cup

½ cup firmly packed dark brown sugar
5 tablespoons fresh orange juice, divided
2 tablespoons butter
1 cup confectioners' sugar, sifted
1 teaspoon vanilla extract

1. In a medium saucepan, combine brown sugar, 3 tablespoons orange juice, and butter. Bring to a simmer over medium heat. Reduce heat to low; simmer 2 minutes, stirring occasionally. Remove from heat. Pour into a medium bowl. Gradually add confectioners' sugar, beating at medium speed with a mixer until combined (about 30 seconds). Beat in vanilla. (If mixture is too thick, add enough of remaining orange juice, 1 tablespoon at a time, until a drizzle consistency is achieved.) Use immediately.

Cranberry-Cider Fizz
Makes about 12 servings

1 (64-ounce) bottle cranberry juice cocktail, chilled
1 (750-milliliter) bottle sparkling apple cider, chilled
3 cups fresh orange juice
¼ cup fresh lime juice
Garnish: apple slices, orange slices, lime slices, and cranberries

1. In a large pitcher, combine cranberry juice, cider, orange juice, and lime juice. Serve over ice. Garnish with apple slices, orange slices, lime slices, and cranberries, if desired. Serve immediately.

Christmas, Buffet Style

WHEN THE HOUSE IS FULL OF THOSE MOST DEAR, IT'S IMPORTANT TO CATCH UP AND SPEND TIME WITH ONE ANOTHER. A BUFFET-STYLE CHRISTMAS IS A PRACTICAL WAY TO ENJOY THE GATHERING.

On the Menu

SAUSAGE BREAKFAST CASSEROLE
HOT CURRIED FRUIT
DOUBLE CHEESE GRITS CASSEROLE
SWEET POTATO-PECAN MUFFINS
CRANBERRY SPLASH

Sweet Potato-Pecan Muffins

Makes 14 muffins

1⅔ cups all-purpose flour
1 teaspoon baking soda
¼ teaspoon baking powder
¾ teaspoon salt
¾ teaspoon ground cinnamon
¼ teaspoon ground nutmeg
½ cup chopped pecans
⅓ cup vegetable shortening
1⅓ cups sugar
2 large eggs
1 (15-ounce) can sweet potatoes,
   drained and mashed
⅓ cup water

1. Preheat oven to 350°. Spray muffin pans with nonstick cooking spray.

2. In a large bowl, combine flour, baking soda, baking powder, salt, cinnamon, nutmeg, and pecans; make a well in center of mixture.

3. In a medium bowl, beat shortening at medium speed with a mixer until creamy; gradually add sugar, beating until fluffy. Add eggs, one at a time, beating after each addition. Add mashed sweet potatoes and water, beating well. Add to dry ingredients; stir just until moistened.

4. Spoon batter into prepared muffin pans. Bake for 20 to 25 minutes. Cool in pans for 10 minutes. Remove from pans, and cool on wire racks.

CRANBERRY SPLASH

Cranberry Splash

Makes 1 gallon

8 cups cranberry juice cocktail, chilled
8 cups pineapple-orange juice, chilled

1. In a large pitcher, combine cranberry juice and pineapple-orange juice , stirring well. Serve over ice, if desired.

Hot Curried Fruit

Makes 10 servings

1 (29-ounce) can peach halves, drained
1 (29-ounce) can pear halves, drained
1 (20-ounce) can pineapple chunks, drained
1 (15¼-ounce) can apricot halves, drained
1 (6-ounce) jar maraschino cherries without stems, drained
½ cup butter, melted
¾ cup firmly packed brown sugar
2 tablespoons all-purpose flour
1 teaspoon curry powder

1. Preheat oven to 350°. Spray a 13x9-inch baking dish with nonstick cooking spray.

2. In a large bowl, combine peaches, pears, pineapple, apricots, and cherries. Pour melted butter over fruit. In a small bowl, combine brown sugar, flour, and curry powder; add to fruit,

stirring gently. Spoon mixture into prepared baking dish. Cover and bake for 30 minutes or until thoroughly heated.

Double Cheese Grits Casserole

Makes 8 servings

2½ cups milk
2 cups water
½ teaspoon salt
1 cup regular grits, uncooked
2 cups shredded Cheddar cheese
½ cup grated Parmesan cheese
½ cup butter
2 large eggs
Paprika

1. Preheat oven to 350°. Spray a 2-quart baking dish with nonstick cooking spray.

2. In a large saucepan, combine milk, water, and salt; bring to a boil. Stir in grits. Cover, reduce heat, and simmer for 15 minutes, stirring occasionally. Add Cheddar and Parmesan cheeses and butter. Stir until cheeses and butter melt.

3. In a small bowl, beat eggs with a fork. Gradually stir in a small amount of hot grits mixture into beaten eggs. Add egg mixture to remaining hot grits mixture in saucepan, stirring constantly. Pour into prepared baking dish. Sprinkle with paprika. Bake, uncovered, for 40 to 45 minutes or until set and golden.

Sausage Breakfast Casserole

Makes 8 servings

1 (8-ounce) can refrigerated crescent rolls
1 pound ground pork sausage
1 cup shredded Cheddar cheese
1 cup shredded mozzarella cheese
6 large eggs, lightly beaten
1½ cups milk
½ teaspoon salt
Garnish: tomato wedges and fresh parsley

1. Preheat oven to 375°. Spray a 13x9-inch baking dish with nonstick cooking spray.

2. Unroll crescent rolls. Place in bottom of prepared baking dish, pressing perforations together to seal and form a crust. Bake for 6 minutes. (Crust will be puffy.) Remove from oven, and set aside. Reduce oven temperature to 350°.

3. In a large skillet, cook sausage over medium heat until browned and crumbly. Drain, spoon over baked crust, and sprinkle with cheeses.

4. In a medium bowl, combine eggs, milk, and salt; pour over cheese. Bake for 35 to 40 minutes or until top is golden brown. Garnish with tomato wedges and fresh parsley, if desired.

A Grand Evening

STRIKING CANDLESTICKS, DELICATE ORNAMENTS, AND VIVID GREENERY FASHION A WELCOMING HOLIDAY ATMOSPHERE, ESPECIALLY WHEN A BEAUTIFUL WINTER WONDERLAND CAN BE GLIMPSED THROUGH THE WINDOWS. TEMPT GUESTS WITH A MENU AS NOTABLE AS THE DÉCOR, INCLUDING FLAVORFUL CASSOULET, ROASTED VEGETABLES, AND TO-DIE-FOR CHOCOLATE DESSERTS.

On the Menu

Seasonal Spinach Salad
Makes 10 to 12 servings

2 (6-ounce) bags fresh baby spinach
1 (5-ounce) bag spring mix
1½ cups toasted walnut halves
2 (4-ounce) packages blue cheese
   crumbles
½ cup pomegranate seeds
2 red pears, sliced
1½ teaspoons kosher salt
¾ teaspoon ground black pepper
Lemon-Honey Vinaigrette
   (recipe follows)

1. In a large bowl, combine spinach, spring mix, walnuts, cheese, seeds, and pears. Season with salt and pepper. Drizzle with desired amount of vinaigrette; serve immediately.

Lemon-Honey Vinaigrette
Makes about 2½ cups

½ cup white wine vinegar
¼ cup fresh lemon juice
3 tablespoons honey
2 tablespoons chopped fresh
   parsley
2 tablespoons chopped fresh chives
1 tablespoon chopped fresh shallot
1½ teaspoons kosher salt
¾ teaspoon ground black pepper
1½ cups extra-virgin olive oil

1. In a small bowl, whisk together vinegar, juice, and honey. Add herbs, shallot, salt, and pepper. Chill for at least 1 hour. Add olive oil, whisking to combine. Serve immediately, or store, covered, in refrigerator for up to 2 days.

Brussels Sprouts with Bacon and Pearl Onions
Makes 10 to 12 servings

1 (12-ounce) package center-cut
   bacon
4 pounds Brussels sprouts, outer
   leaves and stems removed,
   cut in half
1 (16-ounce) bag frozen pearl
   onions, thawed
1 cup water
¼ cup unsalted butter
1 teaspoon sugar
1 teaspoon kosher salt
½ teaspoon ground black pepper
Garnish: fresh thyme and chopped
   fresh parsley

1. In a Dutch oven, cook bacon over medium-high heat until browned; remove from pan, and drain, discarding drippings. Crumble bacon and set aside. Add Brussels sprouts, onions, water, butter, sugar, salt, and pepper to pan. Simmer over medium-high heat, stirring occasionally, until almost all water is evaporated (about 15 minutes). Add reserved bacon. Cook for 2 minutes. Serve immediately. Garnish with fresh thyme and chopped parsley, if desired.

Pork and Sausage Cassoulet
Makes 10 to 12 servings

3 tablespoons olive oil
5 to 6 pork loin chops, cut in half
    lengthwise
1 tablespoon kosher salt,
    divided
1 tablespoon freshly ground black
    pepper, divided
1 pound smoked beef sausage,
    sliced ¼-inch thick
1 medium red onion, peeled and
    chopped
1 small butternut squash, peeled,
    seeded, and chopped
6 cloves garlic, peeled
⅔ cup sherry
1½ quarts chicken broth
3 bay leaves
3 (15-ounce) cans great Northern
    beans
¼ cup cornstarch
¼ cup cold water

1. In a large Dutch oven, heat oil over medium-high heat. Season pork with 1½ teaspoons salt and 1½ teaspoons pepper. Add pork; cook 3 to 5 minutes per side or until browned; remove from pan, and set aside. In same pan, brown sausage, and set aside.

2. Add onion, squash, and garlic; cook until onion is tender (about 10 minutes). Stir in sherry, and cook 2 to 3 minutes, scraping browned bits from bottom of pan with a wooden spoon. Cook, stirring occasionally, until mixture is reduced and thickened (about 5 minutes). Increase heat to high. Add broth, remaining 1½ teaspoons salt, remaining 1½ teaspoons pepper, bay leaves, pork, and sausage. Bring mixture to a boil; reduce heat, and cover. Simmer mixture over medium heat for about 20 minutes. Add beans, and cook 5 minutes longer.

3. In a small bowl, whisk together cornstarch and water. Add to pork mixture, stirring to combine. Cook until thickened, stirring frequently, about 5 minutes. Remove from heat, and serve.

Whole Wheat Parmesan Rolls with Herb Butter

Makes 10 to 12 servings

2 (15.8-ounce) packages frozen
  whole wheat rolls, thawed*
Herb Butter (recipe follows)
½ cup grated Parmesan cheese

1. Preheat oven according to package directions. Spread about 1 tablespoon herb butter onto each roll; sprinkle with about 1 tablespoon cheese.

2. Bake according to package directions. Serve warm with additional Herb Butter, if desired.

*We used Sister Schubert's.

Herb Butter

Makes 1⅓ cups

1 cup butter, softened
2 tablespoons chopped fresh
  rosemary
2 tablespoons chopped fresh parsley
2 tablespoons chopped fresh sage
1 teaspoon garlic salt
½ teaspoon ground black pepper

1. In a medium bowl, beat butter at medium speed with a mixer until creamy, about 2 minutes. Add rosemary, parsley, sage, garlic salt, and pepper. Use immediately, or store, covered, in refrigerator for up to 3 days.

Roasted Root Vegetables with Rosemary
Makes 10 to 12 servings

1 (3-pound) package red potatoes,
  cut into quarters
4 (6-ounce) packages baby rainbow
  carrots, cut in half
1 (1-pound) package parsnips,
  peeled and cut into 2-inch pieces
6 cloves garlic, peeled
4 shallots, peeled and cut into
  quarters
⅓ cup olive oil
¼ cup chopped fresh rosemary
1 tablespoon kosher salt
2½ teaspoons ground black pepper

1. Preheat oven to 400°. Line 2 rimmed baking sheets with aluminum foil; set aside.

2. In a large bowl, combine potatoes, carrots, parsnips, garlic, shallots, and oil. Divide mixture between prepared pans. Sprinkle with rosemary, salt, and pepper.

3. Bake for 45 minutes, stirring occasionally. Cool slightly before serving.

Chocolate Mousse Pie

Makes 1 (10-inch) pie

2½ cups chocolate graham cracker
    crumbs
1 cup sugar
½ cup butter, melted
1½ cups cold milk

1 (3.4-ounce) box instant chocolate-
    flavored pudding mix
1 cup heavy whipping cream
3 teaspoons unflavored gelatin
1 (16-ounce) container frozen
    whipped topping, thawed
Garnish: chocolate curls

1. Spray a 10-inch springform pan
with nonstick baking spray with flour;
line the bottom with parchment
paper, and spray again; set aside. In
a large bowl, combine crumbs and
sugar. Add butter, and stir to combine.
Press mixture into the bottom of
prepared pan; place in freezer for
about 15 minutes.

2. In a large bowl, whisk together
milk and pudding mix until smooth
and thickened (about 1 minute).

3. In a small saucepan, combine
cream and gelatin; let mixture stand
for 3 minutes. Cook mixture over low
heat, whisking constantly, until gelatin
is dissolved and mixture is smooth;
cool slightly. Add gelatin mixture
to pudding mixture, whisking until
combined.

4. Add whipped topping to pudding
mixture, whisking to combine. Spoon
into prepared pan; chill for at least
1 hour. Garnish with chocolate curls, if
desired. Store, covered, in refrigerator
for up to 3 days.

Chocolate Toffee Trifle

Makes 10 to 12 servings

1½ cups cold milk
1 (3.4-ounce) box instant chocolate-
    flavored pudding mix
1 cup heavy whipping cream
3 teaspoons unflavored gelatin
2 (16-ounce) containers frozen
    whipped topping, thawed and
    divided
2 cups chocolate-covered toffee bits
1 prepared angel food cake, cut into
    2-inch cubes

1. In a large bowl, whisk together
milk and pudding mix until smooth
and thickened (about 1 minute).

2. In a small saucepan, combine
cream and gelatin; let mixture stand
for 3 minutes. Cook mixture over low
heat, whisking constantly, until gelatin
is dissolved and mixture is smooth;
cool slightly. Add gelatin mixture
to pudding mixture, whisking until
combined.

3. Add 1 container of whipped
topping to pudding mixture, whisking
to combine. Spoon half of mixture
into the bottom of a large trifle dish;
sprinkle with 1 cup toffee bits. Layer
half of cake onto toffee bits. Repeat
layers. Spoon remaining container of
whipped topping onto cake. Store,
covered, in refrigerator for up to 2 days.

Turkey Tradition

CHRISTMAS IS THE SEASON OF SHARING AND CELEBRATING. AND THERE'S NO BETTER WAY THAN TO HOST A CASUAL DINNER PARTY.

HOLIDAY ITALIAN SALAD
AND EASY ORANGE ROLLS

On the Menu

Holiday Italian Salad
Makes 8 servings

4 cups torn green leaf lettuce
4 cups torn red leaf lettuce
1 cup chopped walnuts, toasted
1 yellow bell pepper, cut into thin
   strips
1 orange bell pepper, cut into thin
   strips
Creamy Balsamic Italian Dressing
   (recipe follows)

1. In a large bowl, combine lettuces, walnuts, and bell peppers. Add dressing, tossing gently. Serve immediately.

Creamy Balsamic Italian Dressing
Makes about 2 cups

1 cup ranch dressing
½ cup olive oil
¼ cup balsamic vinegar
1 (0.7-ounce) envelope zesty Italian
   salad dressing mix
3 tablespoons water

1. In a small bowl, combine ranch dressing, olive oil, vinegar, dressing mix, and water; whisk until well blended. Cover and chill for 1 hour. Whisk well before serving.

Squash and Zucchini Casserole
Makes 12 to 16 servings

½ cup plus 2 tablespoons butter,
   divided
6 medium zucchini, thinly sliced
4 medium yellow squash, thinly
   sliced
1 (8-ounce) package sliced fresh
   mushrooms
1 onion, chopped
1 teaspoon salt
1 teaspoon ground black pepper
1 sleeve round buttery crackers,
   crushed
½ cup grated Parmesan cheese

1. In a large skillet over medium-high heat, melt ½ cup butter. Add vegetables; cook, uncovered, for 20 minutes or until tender, stirring often. Add salt and pepper.

2. Preheat oven to 350°.

3. Spray a 13x9-inch baking dish with nonstick cooking spray. Spoon squash mixture into prepared baking dish; set aside.

4. In a medium saucepan over low heat, melt remaining 2 tablespoons butter. Remove from heat. Stir in crushed crackers and cheese. Sprinkle mixture over casserole.

5. Bake for 45 minutes or until hot and bubbly.

Glazed Carrots
Makes 8 to 12 servings

2 pounds baby carrots
3 tablespoons butter
½ cup firmly packed brown sugar
¼ cup fresh orange juice
2 teaspoons cornstarch
½ teaspoon orange zest
¼ teaspoon ground ginger
¼ teaspoon salt

1. In a large saucepan, add carrots and water to cover. Bring to a boil over high heat. Reduce heat to low, cover, and cook for 10 minutes or until tender. Drain well. Set aside, and keep warm.

2. In a small saucepan, combine butter, sugar, orange juice, cornstarch, orange zest, and ginger. Cook over medium heat, stirring constantly, until mixture boils. Boil for 1 minute, stirring constantly. Remove from heat; stir in salt. Pour mixture over carrots; toss well.

Deep-fried Turkey

Makes 1 (13-pound) turkey

2 teaspoons dried oregano
2 teaspoons dried basil
1 teaspoon dried parsley
1 teaspoon salt
1 teaspoon ground black pepper
1 (13-pound) turkey
3 to 4 gallons peanut oil
Garnish: fresh parsley and sage

1. In a small bowl, combine oregano, basil, parsley, salt, and pepper; set aside.

2. Remove and discard giblets and neck from turkey. Remove and discard plastic ring holding legs together and pop-up timer. Loosen skin from breast without totally detaching it; carefully rub spice mixture under skin, and replace skin. Let stand for 30 minutes before frying.

3. Heat peanut oil in propane turkey fryer to 375° over medium-low flame, following manufacturer's instructions. (See box at right for step-by-step instructions.) Place turkey in fryer basket. Carefully lower basket into hot oil. Temperature should drop and remain at 325°. Cook for about 45 minutes (3½ minutes per pound at 325°). Slowly remove basket from oil. Drain and cool slightly before slicing.

4. Garnish with fresh parsley and sage, if desired.

Handy Tips for Deep-fried Turkey

Fried turkey is a delicious Southern tradition that happens to be easy, too. However, there are a few safety tips to keep in mind:

- *Always fry outdoors.*
- *Never leave frying turkey unattended.*
- *Have a fire extinguisher handy.*
- *Allow oil to cool completely before moving fryer and discarding oil.*

STEP-BY-STEP

[1] Place turkey in fryer basket, lower basket into fryer, and fill with peanut oil to 1 inch above turkey.

[2] Remove turkey and fryer basket, and let drain on pan lined with paper towels. Light propane burner.

[3] Heat oil to 375° over medium-low flame. This will take 30 to 45 minutes.

[4] Using an oven mitt and the fryer hook, very slowly lower fryer basket with turkey into hot oil to avoid spillage.

[5] Cover fryer, and insert thermometer in lid. Temperature should drop and remain at 325°. Adjust propane flame as needed to maintain temperature.

[6] Fry turkey for 3½ minutes per pound. Meat thermometer inserted in thigh should register 180°. To avoid starting a fire, turn off propane before removing turkey from fryer. Using an oven mitt and the fryer hook, very slowly lift fryer basket. Drain over fryer before removing turkey.

Broccoli and Cheese Stuffed Potatoes

Makes 10 servings

10 large baking potatoes
1 (16-ounce) container sour cream
1 (8-ounce) package cream cheese, softened
¼ cup butter
2 teaspoons salt
1 teaspoon ground black pepper
3 cups fresh broccoli florets, cooked until crisp-tender
1 cup shredded Colby-Jack cheese blend

1. Preheat oven to 425°.

2. Rinse potatoes, and wrap in aluminum foil. Place on a baking sheet. Bake for 1 hour or until done. Set aside potatoes until cool enough to handle. Reduce oven temperature to 350°.

3. Cut off top one-third of potatoes lengthwise, and scoop out pulp, leaving ¼-inch-thick shells.

4. In a large bowl, mash potato pulp. Add sour cream, cream cheese, butter, salt, and pepper, stirring until well blended. Add broccoli, stirring gently. Spoon potato-broccoli mixture into potato shells.

5. Place potatoes on baking sheet. Bake for 30 minutes. Sprinkle tops with shredded cheese. Bake for 10 minutes longer.

Cornbread Dressing

Makes 12 to 16 servings

2 (6-ounce) packages buttermilk cornbread mix
½ cup butter
2 cups chopped onion
2 cups chopped celery
2 cups crumbled biscuits
1 tablespoon poultry seasoning
1 teaspoon salt
4½ cups chicken broth
1 (10¾-ounce) can cream of chicken soup
3 large eggs, beaten

1. Bake cornbread mix according to package directions. Cool and crumble.

2. Preheat oven to 350°. Spray a 13x9-inch baking dish with nonstick cooking spray.

3. In a large skillet over medium-high heat, melt butter. Add onion and celery; cook, stirring constantly, for 7 minutes or until tender.

4. In a large bowl, combine crumbled cornbread and biscuits, poultry seasoning, and salt; stir in vegetable mixture. Add broth, soup, and eggs, stirring well. Pour mixture into prepared baking dish. Bake for 45 to 50 minutes or until center is set.

Easy Orange Rolls

Makes 36 rolls

6 tablespoons butter, melted
3 tablespoons fresh orange juice
1 teaspoon orange zest
1 (3-pound) package frozen roll dough, thawed
Orange Glaze (recipe follows)

1. In a small bowl, stir together melted butter, orange juice, and zest; set aside.

2. Spray 3 (12-cup) muffin pans with nonstick cooking spray.

3. Divide each roll into 3 equal parts; roll into balls. Dip each ball into butter

mixture. Place 3 balls into each muffin cup. Cover and let rise in a warm place (85°), free from drafts, until doubled in size, about 2 hours.

4. Preheat oven to 350°. Bake for 10 to 12 minutes or until lightly browned. Drizzle with Orange Glaze.

Orange Glaze
Makes about 1 cup

1½ cups confectioners' sugar
3 tablespoons fresh orange juice

1. Combine sugar and orange juice, stirring until smooth.

White Chocolate Mousse Cake
Makes 1 (9-inch) cake

2 (3-ounce) packages ladyfingers, split
¾ cup milk
30 large marshmallows
6 (1-ounce) squares white chocolate
2 cups heavy whipping cream
Strawberry Sauce (recipe follows)
Garnish: chocolate-dipped strawberries

1. Line bottom and sides of a 9-inch springform pan with ladyfingers, cut sides in; set aside.

2. In a heavy saucepan, combine milk, marshmallows, and chocolate. Cook over low heat, stirring constantly,

until smooth. Remove from heat. Cool for 20 minutes.

3. In a large bowl, beat whipping cream at high speed with a mixer until soft peaks form. Gently fold into cooled chocolate mixture.

4. Pour chocolate mixture into prepared pan. Cover and chill for at least 4 hours. Serve with Strawberry Sauce.

5. Garnish with chocolate-dipped strawberries, if desired.

Strawberry Sauce
Makes 1½ cups

1 (10-ounce) package frozen sliced strawberries, thawed
2 teaspoons cornstarch
½ cup light corn syrup
1 teaspoon lemon juice

1. In a small saucepan, combine strawberries, cornstarch, corn syrup, and lemon juice. Cook over medium heat, stirring constantly, until mixture boils. Boil for 1 minute, stirring constantly. Remove from heat; cool before serving.

Christmas Tidings

JOYFUL TRADITIONS CALL FOR SATISFYING SAVORIES, TASTY SWEETS, AND THE ENJOYABLE CONVERSATION OF FRIENDS AND NEIGHBORS. A CROWN PORK ROAST IS TRULY FIT FOR A KING, AND OUR DELECTABLE DUO OF SWEET POTATO LAYER CAKE AND CHOCOLATE CAKE ROLL ARE A DELIGHTFUL FINISH.

On the Menu

Warm Baby Spinach, Bacon, and Green Bean Salad
Apple-glazed Crown Pork Roast   Wild Rice with Cranberries
Herb and Parmesan Biscuits
Sweet Potato Layer Cake with Molasses Frosting
Chocolate Cake Roll with Fig Filling and Kumquat-Pineapple Syrup

Warm Baby Spinach, Bacon, and Green Bean Salad
Makes about 8 servings

½ pound fresh haricots verts, trimmed
3 strips bacon
1 (8-ounce) package white button mushrooms, quartered
½ cup thinly sliced red onion
½ cup prepared olive oil and vinegar dressing*
1 (6-ounce) bag fresh baby spinach

1. In a large saucepan, cook beans in boiling water for 3 minutes; drain. Pat beans dry with a paper towel. In a large skillet, cook bacon over medium heat until crisp. Remove bacon, reserving drippings in skillet, and drain on paper towels; crumble bacon. Add mushrooms and onion to skillet; cook over medium-high heat for 3 minutes or until mushrooms begin to brown. Add beans; cook for 2 minutes or until warmed. Stir in dressing.

2. In a large serving bowl, place spinach; add hot mushroom mixture, tossing well. Sprinkle with crumbled bacon. Serve immediately.

Note: Haricots verts are small, slender, delicately flavored young green beans. They're also called French green beans.

*We used Newman's Own.

Apple-glazed Crown Pork Roast
Makes 8 to 10 servings

¾ cup apple jelly
3 tablespoons apple cider vinegar
1 tablespoon maple syrup
1 tablespoon water
1 teaspoon soy sauce
1 (16-rib) crown roast of pork, trimmed
2 tablespoons olive oil
2 teaspoons kosher salt
1 teaspoon freshly ground black pepper
Garnish: fresh herbs, kumquats, and Sautéed Lady Apples (recipe follows)

1. Preheat oven to 350°. In a small saucepan, combine jelly, vinegar, syrup, water, and soy sauce. Bring to a simmer over medium heat. Reduce heat to medium-low; cook for 5 minutes or until smooth, stirring frequently. Cover and set aside.

2. Spray the rack of a broiler pan with nonstick cooking spray; place rack on broiler pan. Place pork on rack. Brush pork with olive oil; sprinkle with salt

and pepper. Pour 2 cups water into broiler pan. Cover tips of ribs with foil.

3. Bake pork for 2 hours and 30 minutes or until a meat thermometer inserted in thickest portion registers 145° or until desired degree of doneness, basting occasionally with apple jelly mixture during last hour of baking time. Add additional water to pan if necessary during baking. Remove from oven; let stand for 15 minutes, and remove foil from tips of ribs before serving. Place pork on a platter; garnish with fresh herbs, kumquats, and Sautéed Lady Apples, if desired.

Note: Ask the butcher to trim and tie the roast.

Sautéed Lady Apples

1. Cut 4 small Lady apples in half. In a large skillet, heat 1 tablespoon canola oil over medium-high heat. Place apple halves, cut sides down, in skillet. Cook until lightly browned, about 2 or 3 minutes per side. (To substitute Gala apples for Lady apples, core Gala apples, and cut into wedges before cooking.)

Herb and Parmesan Biscuits

Makes about 30 biscuits

4 cups all-purpose flour
2 tablespoons grated Parmesan cheese
1 tablespoon baking powder
1 tablespoon finely chopped fresh sage
1 tablespoon finely chopped fresh rosemary
1½ teaspoons salt
¼ teaspoon ground black pepper
1 cup chilled butter, cut into small pieces
1 cup plus 3 tablespoons whole milk, divided
3 large eggs, divided
1 teaspoon water

1. Preheat oven to 425°. Line a large baking sheet with parchment paper. In the work bowl of a food processor, combine flour, cheese, baking powder, sage, rosemary, salt, and pepper; pulse 3 times. Add chilled butter; pulse 3 or 4 times or until mixture is crumbly. Spoon mixture into a large bowl; make a well in center of mixture. In a small bowl, whisk together 1 cup milk and 2 eggs. Add egg mixture to dry ingredients; stir until dry ingredients are moistened (add remaining 3 tablespoons milk, if necessary). Place dough on a lightly floured surface; knead 2 or 3 times.

2. Roll dough to about ½-inch thickness. Using a fluted 2-inch biscuit cutter dipped in flour, cut out dough.

Reroll scraps if necessary. Place on prepared baking sheet. In a small bowl, whisk together remaining egg and water; lightly brush over tops of dough. Bake for about 12 minutes or until golden brown.

Wild Rice with Cranberries

Makes about 10 servings

2 tablespoons butter
1 cup chopped carrot
½ cup chopped celery
1 (16-ounce) package wild and whole-grain brown rice blend*
4¾ cups chicken broth
¾ teaspoon salt
½ teaspoon ground black pepper
1 cup sweetened dried cranberries
2 tablespoons chopped parsley

1. In a large skillet, melt butter over medium-high heat. Add carrots and celery; cook for 5 minutes or until vegetables begin to soften. Add rice; cook for 1 minute. Stir in broth, salt, and pepper; bring to a boil. Reduce heat to medium-low; cover and simmer for 45 to 50 minutes or until most of liquid is absorbed. Stir in cranberries; cover and let stand for 10 minutes. Sprinkle with parsley.

*We used Lundberg Wild Blend rice.

Chocolate Cake Roll with Fig Filling and Kumquat-Pineapple Syrup

Makes 1 (10-inch) cake roll

¾ cup plus 3 tablespoons all-
  purpose flour, divided
¼ cup plus 3 tablespoons
  unsweetened cocoa powder,
  divided
3 large eggs
1 cup sugar
1 teaspoon baking powder
¼ teaspoon baking soda
¼ teaspoon salt
⅓ cup water
1 teaspoon vanilla extract
Kumquat-Pineapple Syrup
  (recipe follows)
Fig Filling (recipe follows)
Garnish: unsweetened cocoa powder
  and cinnamon sticks

1. Preheat oven to 350°. Spray a rimmed 15x10-inch baking pan with nonstick cooking spray. Line bottom of pan with wax paper. Spray wax paper with cooking spray; dust with 3 tablespoons flour, shaking off excess. Sift 3 tablespoons cocoa powder evenly over a large clean kitchen towel.

2. In a large bowl, combine eggs and sugar. Beat at high speed with a mixer until thick and pale, about 5 minutes. Sift remaining ¾ cup flour, remaining ¼ cup cocoa powder, baking powder, baking soda, and salt over egg mixture; add water and vanilla. Beat at low speed just until combined. Pour batter into prepared pan, spreading to edges.

3. Bake for 12 to 14 minutes or until cake springs back when lightly touched in center. Using a sharp knife, loosen edges of cake from pan. Invert warm cake onto prepared towel. Gently peel off wax paper. Starting on one short side, roll up cake and towel together, and cool completely on a wire rack, about 2 hours.

4. Unroll cake, and gently remove towel. Remove 3 tablespoons liquid mixture from Kumquat-Pineapple Syrup, reserving remaining syrup; brush cake with liquid mixture. Spread Fig Filling over cake, leaving a ½-inch border. Roll up cake, starting at one short side. Place roll, seam-side down, on a sheet of plastic wrap; wrap tightly. Chill for at least 2 hours or up to 6 hours. Remove plastic wrap from roll, and place on a serving platter, seam-side down. Garnish with cocoa powder over the top, if desired. Serve with reserved Kumquat-Pineapple Syrup and garnish with additional cinnamon sticks, if desired.

Kumquat-Pineapple Syrup

Makes about 3 cups

1 cup water
1 cup sugar
Dash of salt
1½ cups coarsely chopped
  fresh pineapple
½ cup sliced kumquats
2 tablespoons fig preserves
2 cinnamon sticks, broken in half

1. In a medium saucepan, combine water, sugar, and salt; stir to moisten sugar. Bring to a boil, without stirring. Reduce heat; simmer for 5 minutes, without stirring. Remove from heat; stir in pineapple, kumquats, preserves, and cinnamon sticks. Pour into a bowl; cover and chill about 2 hours. Discard cinnamon sticks before serving.

Fig Filling

Makes about 3 cups

4 ounces cream cheese, softened
⅓ cup fig preserves
1¼ cups chilled heavy whipping cream

1. In a large bowl, combine cream cheese and preserves. Beat at medium speed with a mixer until blended. Add chilled whipping cream; beat at low speed until mixture begins to thicken. Increase speed to high, and beat until thickened (do not overbeat).

Note: If using a heavy-duty stand mixer, use the whisk attachment to beat in cream.

Fruity Favorite A favorite jar of preserves is versatile, whether spread on your toast at breakfast or added to cake fillings or syrups for a more distinct flavor. Next time you are at your local farmers' market or specialty store, be sure to purchase a couple to take home.

Sweet Potato Layer Cake with Molasses Frosting

Makes 1 (9-inch) cake

¾ cup butter, softened
⅔ cup sugar
⅔ cup firmly packed dark brown
  sugar
3 large eggs
1 (15-ounce) can cut sweet potatoes
  in syrup, undrained
⅓ cup whole milk
1 teaspoon vanilla extract
2⅔ cups all-purpose flour
2½ teaspoons baking powder
1 teaspoon pumpkin pie spice
½ teaspoon salt
¼ teaspoon baking soda
Sweet Potato Filling (recipe follows)
Molasses Frosting (recipe follows)
Pecan Topping (recipe follows)

1. Preheat oven to 350°. Lightly spray 2 (9-inch) round cake pans with nonstick baking spray with flour; line with parchment paper rounds, and spray again.

2. In a large bowl, combine butter and sugars; beat at medium speed with a mixer until fluffy. Add eggs, one at a time, beating well after each addition. In a medium bowl, combine undrained sweet potatoes, milk, and vanilla; coarsely mash using a potato masher. In a large bowl, whisk together flour, baking powder, pumpkin pie spice, salt, and baking soda. With mixer on low speed,

add flour mixture to butter mixture alternately with sweet potato mixture, beginning and ending with flour mixture. Beat just until combined after each addition. Divide batter between prepared pans; smooth tops.

3. Bake for 25 to 27 minutes or until a wooden pick inserted in center comes out clean. Let cool in pans on a wire rack for 10 minutes. Invert cakes onto wire rack, and gently remove parchment paper. Cool cake layers completely.

4. Place one cake layer on a rimmed cake plate; spread Sweet Potato Filling over layer. Top with remaining cake layer; gently press. Run a spatula around sides to remove any excess filling, if necessary. Spread Molasses Frosting over top and sides of cake. Just before serving, spoon Pecan Topping over cake.

Sweet Potato Filling

Makes about 2 cups

1 (15-ounce) can cut sweet potatoes
  in syrup, drained
4 ounces cream cheese, softened
⅓ cup confectioners' sugar
½ teaspoon pumpkin pie spice
¼ cup chilled heavy whipping
  cream

1. In a large bowl, combine drained sweet potatoes and cream cheese; beat at medium speed with a mixer until well blended, scraping bowl occasionally. Beat in confectioners'

sugar and pumpkin pie spice. Add whipping cream; beat at high speed just until thickened and fluffy.

Molasses Frosting

Makes about 3 cups

½ cup butter, softened
4 ounces cream cheese, softened
3 tablespoons molasses
6 cups confectioners' sugar, sifted
4 to 6 tablespoons whole milk

1. In a large bowl, beat butter and cream cheese at medium speed with a mixer until smooth. Beat in molasses. Gradually beat in confectioners' sugar and enough milk for spreading consistency, beating until combined.

Pecan Topping

Makes about ⅔ cup

½ cup firmly packed dark brown
  sugar
¼ cup water
⅛ teaspoon salt
½ cup pecan halves, toasted

1. In a small saucepan, combine brown sugar, water, and salt; stir to moisten sugar. Bring to a boil over medium-high heat, without stirring. Reduce heat to medium-low; simmer, without stirring, for 4 minutes. Stir in pecans. Cool completely.

Note: If pecan mixture becomes too thick after cooling, stir in 1 tablespoon dark corn syrup.

Sophisticated Holiday

INTIMATE GATHERINGS IN YOUR HOME CREATE MEMORABLE OCCASIONS FOR YEARS TO COME. CHIC DETAILS SUCH AS MONOGRAMMED FINE CHINA, GLEAMING CRYSTAL, AND INTRICATE WOODEN PLACE MATS SET THE TONE FOR A FORMAL HOLIDAY FUNCTION PERFECT FOR ENTERTAINING.

On the Menu

CREAMY APPLE SOUP   ORANGE, OLIVE, AND WATERCRESS SALAD
SPINACH, PROSCIUTTO, AND ROASTED RED PEPPER QUICHE
PARMESAN DILL ROLLS
CHOCOLATE POUND CAKE WITH MINT ICING   CREAMY MIXED BERRIES
CRANBERRY APPLE TEA

Creamy Apple Soup
Makes 8 to 10 servings

4 Braeburn apples, peeled, cored, and chopped
2 Granny Smith apples, peeled, cored, and chopped
1 (32-ounce) carton chicken broth
½ cup half-and-half
1 teaspoon salt
1 cup crème fraîche
Garnish: green onion and apple slices

1. In a large stockpot, combine apples and chicken broth. Bring to a boil over high heat. Reduce heat to medium-low. Cover and cook for 20 minutes or until apples are very tender. Remove from heat, and cool for 10 minutes.

2. In the container of a blender, purée apple mixture in batches until smooth. Return apple mixture to stockpot. Add half-and-half and salt to apple mixture, stirring well. Heat over medium heat for 4 to 5 minutes or until warm, stirring often. Dollop each serving of soup with crème fraîche. Garnish with green onion and apple slices, if desired.

Orange, Olive, and Watercress Salad
Makes 8 servings

8 cups watercress, rinsed, dried, and large stems trimmed
1½ cups Homemade Croutons (recipe follows)
1 cup pitted whole black olives, sliced
½ cup crumbled goat cheese
⅓ cup sliced radishes
2 oranges, peeled and sectioned, juice reserved
⅓ cup white wine vinegar
⅓ cup extra-virgin olive oil
1 teaspoon salt
½ teaspoon ground black pepper

1. In a large bowl, combine watercress, croutons, olives, goat cheese, radishes, and orange sections.

2. In a medium bowl, whisk together reserved orange juice, vinegar, olive oil, salt, and pepper. Pour over salad, tossing gently to coat. Serve immediately.

Homemade Croutons
Makes 6 cups

6 cups (¾-inch) sourdough bread cubes
¼ cup extra-virgin olive oil
2 teaspoons salt
2 teaspoons ground black pepper

1. Preheat oven to 400°.

2. In a large bowl, combine bread, olive oil, salt, and pepper, tossing gently to coat. Spread in an even layer on a rimmed baking sheet. Bake for 7 minutes or until lightly golden.

Spinach, Prosciutto, and Roasted Red Pepper Quiche
Makes 1 (9-inch) quiche

1 tablespoon extra-virgin olive oil
1 (6-ounce) bag fresh baby spinach
½ (14.1-ounce) package refrigerated
   pie crusts
6 slices prosciutto, chopped
⅓ cup chopped roasted red pepper,
   patted dry with paper towels
8 large eggs
2 tablespoons whipping cream
½ teaspoon salt
½ teaspoon ground black pepper

1. Preheat oven to 400°.

2. In a large sauté pan, heat olive oil over medium heat. Add spinach to pan. Cook for 4 to 6 minutes or until spinach is wilted. Cool for 5 minutes or until cool enough to handle. Squeeze excess water from spinach.

3. On a baking sheet, place 1 (9-inch) round removable-bottom tart pan.

4. Unroll pie crust. Press crust into bottom and up sides of tart pan. Spread spinach, prosciutto, and roasted red pepper over pie crust.

5. In a large bowl, whisk together eggs, cream, salt, and pepper. Pour over spinach mixture in pie crust. Bake for 25 to 30 minutes or until center of quiche is set, covering with foil if necessary to prevent excessive browning. Cool in

pan for 20 minutes. Remove from pan, and cool completely on a wire rack.

Parmesan Dill Rolls
Makes 12 rolls

3 cups self-rising flour
¾ cup shredded Parmesan cheese,
   divided
⅓ cup mayonnaise
2 tablespoons chopped fresh dill
1 tablespoon chopped fresh
   chives
1½ cups buttermilk

1. Preheat oven to 425°. Spray a 12-cup muffin pan with nonstick baking spray with flour.

2. In a large bowl, combine flour, ½ cup Parmesan cheese, mayonnaise, dill, and chives, stirring well. Add buttermilk, stirring until smooth. Spoon batter into prepared muffin pan. Sprinkle with remaining ¼ cup Parmesan cheese.

3. Bake for 13 to 15 minutes or until lightly golden. Remove from pan. Serve immediately.

Cranberry Apple Tea
Makes 12 servings

8 cups water
4 orange-flavored tea bags
1 cup sugar
6 cups apple-cranberry juice,
   chilled
2 cups club soda, chilled

1. In a large stockpot, bring 8 cups water to a boil; remove from heat, and add tea bags. Steep for 15 minutes. Remove tea bags, and add sugar, stirring to dissolve. Chill.

2. In a large pitcher, combine tea and apple-cranberry juice, stirring to combine. Add club soda to tea mixture just before serving.

CREAMY MIXED BERRIES

Chocolate Pound Cake with Mint Icing

Makes 12 mini Bundt cakes

1 cup butter, softened
3 cups sugar
5 large eggs
1 teaspoon vanilla extract
2¾ cups all-purpose flour
½ cup unsweetened cocoa powder
½ teaspoon baking powder
¼ teaspoon baking soda
¼ teaspoon salt
1¼ cups buttermilk
Mint Icing (recipe follows)
Garnish: thin crème de menthe
    chocolate mints and whipped
    cream*

1. Preheat oven to 300°. Grease and flour 12 mini Bundt pans, or spray with nonstick baking spray with flour.

2. In a large bowl, combine butter and sugar. Beat at medium-high speed with a mixer until fluffy. Add eggs, one at a time, beating well after each addition. Add vanilla to butter mixture, beating well.

3. In a large bowl, sift together flour, cocoa powder, baking powder, baking soda, and salt. Gradually add flour mixture to butter mixture alternately with buttermilk, beginning and ending with flour mixture, beating to mix well.

4. Pour batter into prepared pans. Bake for 25 to 30 minutes or until a wooden pick inserted in center of cakes comes out clean.

5. Cool in pans for 10 to 15 minutes. Remove from pans, and cool completely on wire racks. Spoon Mint Icing over cakes. Garnish with chocolate mints and whipped cream, if desired.

Note: To make 1 (10-inch) cake, use a 12- to 15-cup Bundt pan. Bake at 300° for 1 hour and 30 minutes or until a wooden pick inserted in center of cake comes out clean.

Mint Icing

Makes about 1 cup

1½ cups confectioners' sugar
2 tablespoons heavy whipping
    cream
2 tablespoons crème de menthe*

1. In a medium bowl, combine confectioners' sugar and whipping cream, whisking well. Add crème de menthe, whisking until smooth. Spoon over cakes. Garnish with chocolate mint shavings and pieces, if desired.

*We used Hiram Walker crème de menthe and Andes mints.

Creamy Mixed Berries

Makes 8 servings

2 cups frozen mixed berries, chopped
2 cups sour cream
2 cups frozen whipped topping,
    thawed
¼ cup confectioners' sugar
Garnish: fresh mint

1. In a large bowl, combine berries, sour cream, whipped topping, and confectioners' sugar, stirring until smooth. Spoon into 8 (4-ounce) ramekins. Garnish with fresh mint, if desired.

Fireside Dining

MAKE A SMALL HOLIDAY GATHERING ESPECIALLY
ENJOYABLE BY PLACING THE DINING TABLE NEAR
THE FIREPLACE. THE FAMILIAR AROMA OF FAVORITE
CHRISTMAS FARE, LOVED ONES SHARING LAUGHTER
AND CONVERSATION AMID THE GLOW OF A COZY
FIRE—THESE ARE THE SIMPLE PLEASURES THAT
WARM OUR HEARTS FOR A LIFETIME.

On the Menu

BUTTERNUT SQUASH, PUMPKIN, AND APPLE SOUP
ROASTED TURKEY WITH SAUSAGE STUFFING   CRANBERRY-ORANGE CHUTNEY
LEMON-THYME GREEN BEANS AND FINGERLING POTATOES
TANGERINE PIE
FROZEN GERMAN CHOCOLATE PIE

Butternut Squash, Pumpkin, and Apple Soup

Makes 6 to 8 servings

1 medium butternut squash,
    cut in half
1 tablespoon olive oil
3 cups peeled, chopped Golden
    Delicious apples
¼ cup chopped shallots
1 teaspoon chopped garlic
1 teaspoon chopped fresh
    rosemary
1 (15-ounce) can pumpkin
2 cups vegetable broth
Garnish: apple slices

1. Preheat oven to 350°. Line a
baking sheet with parchment paper.
Place butternut squash, cut sides
down, on prepared baking sheet.
Bake for 40 minutes or until tender. Cool
for 20 minutes or until cool enough
to handle. Scoop out 1 cup pulp,
reserving remainder for another use.

2. In a Dutch oven, heat oil over
medium-high heat. Add apples,
shallots, and garlic. Sauté for 5 to 6
minutes or until tender. Stir in rosemary.

3. In the container of a blender,
purée 1 cup squash, apple mixture,
and pumpkin. Return purée to Dutch
oven. Slowly add vegetable broth,
stirring until well combined. Cook over
medium heat until heated through.
Garnish with apple slices, if desired.

Roasted Turkey with Sausage Stuffing

Makes 6 to 8 servings

1 pound ground pork sausage
    with sage
1 cup chopped onion
2 cloves garlic, minced
7 cups (1-inch) bread cubes
½ cup chopped dried figs
½ cup halved red grapes
¼ cup chopped fresh parsley
1 cup chicken broth

½ cup butter, softened
1 tablespoon chopped fresh thyme
½ tablespoon chopped fresh rosemary
½ tablespoon kosher salt
1 teaspoon ground black pepper
1 (12- to 14-pound) turkey
Garnish: green and red grapes, fresh
    rosemary, and fresh thyme

1. Preheat oven to 325°.

2. In a large skillet, cook sausage,
onion, and garlic over medium-high
heat, stirring frequently, until browned
and crumbly. Drain, if necessary.*
Return sausage mixture to pan; stir in
bread cubes, figs, grapes, parsley, and
chicken broth.

3. In a medium bowl, combine butter,
thyme, rosemary, salt, and pepper.

4. Stuff sausage mixture into cavity of
turkey. Using butcher's twine, tie legs
together, or, if desired, truss turkey.
Place turkey, breast side up, on rack in
a roasting pan. Rub outside of turkey
with butter mixture.

5. Bake for 4 hours or until a meat
thermometer inserted in thigh and
in center of stuffing registers 165°.
Garnish with grapes, fresh rosemary,
and fresh thyme, if desired.

Note: Sausage-onion mixture can be
cooked ahead. When ready to stuff
turkey, stir in bread cubes, figs, grapes,
parsley, and chicken broth. Stuff
turkey, and rub with butter the day
before you plan to cook it.

Lemon-Thyme Green Beans and Fingerling Potatoes

Makes 6 to 8 servings

2 pounds fingerling potatoes
1 tablespoon salt
2½ pounds green beans, trimmed
½ cup butter, softened
1 tablespoon chopped fresh thyme
1 teaspoon minced garlic
½ cup lemon juice

1. In a large Dutch oven, place potatoes and enough water to cover by 1 inch. Add salt, and bring to a boil. Boil potatoes until tender, about 8 minutes. Using a slotted spoon, place potatoes in a large bowl.

2. Add green beans to boiling water, and cook for 5 to 6 minutes or until tender. Drain; place green beans in bowl with potatoes.

3. In Dutch oven, melt butter over medium heat. Add thyme and garlic, and sauté for 2 minutes or until browned. Stir in lemon juice. Pour butter mixture over green beans and potatoes. Serve immediately.

Note: To make a day ahead, boil potatoes and green beans; plunge into an ice water bath to stop the cooking process. Chill in refrigerator overnight. To heat, arrange on a baking sheet, and place in a 350° oven until heated through. Toss with butter mixture just before serving.

Cranberry-Orange Chutney

Makes 6 to 8 servings

4 cups frozen cranberries
2 cups orange juice
5 tablespoons sugar
2 teaspoons minced fresh ginger
1 tablespoon orange zest
Garnish: orange wedge

1. In a large saucepan, combine cranberries, orange juice, sugar, and ginger. Bring to a boil, and cook until thickened and syrupy, about 14 minutes. Remove from heat, and stir in orange zest. Chill until ready to serve. Garnish with an orange wedge, if desired.

FROZEN GERMAN CHOCOLATE PIE

Frozen German Chocolate Pie

Makes 1 (9-inch) deep-dish pie

½ (14.1-ounce) package refrigerated
    pie crusts
¼ cup butter
3 cups sweetened flaked coconut
1 cup chopped pecans
1 (8-ounce) package cream cheese,
    softened
1 (14-ounce) can sweetened
    condensed milk
2 (4-ounce) dark chocolate bars,
    melted
1 (8-ounce) container frozen extra-
    creamy whipped topping, thawed
½ cup caramel ice-cream topping

1. Preheat oven to 450°. On a lightly
floured surface, roll out dough into
11-inch circle. Fit pie crust into a
(9-inch) deep-dish pie plate; fold
edges under, and crimp. Using a fork,
prick bottom and sides of pie crust.
Bake for 10 minutes or until golden
brown. Cool completely on a wire rack.

2. In a large skillet, melt butter. Stir
in coconut and pecans. Cook for 2 to
3 minutes or until lightly browned.
Remove from heat.

3. In a large bowl, beat cream cheese,
sweetened condensed milk, and
chocolate. Fold in whipped topping.

4. Spoon half of cream cheese
mixture into prepared crust. Top with
¼ cup caramel topping and half of
coconut mixture. Repeat layers with
remaining ingredients. Cover with
plastic wrap, and freeze for at least
4 hours or until firm.

5. Let frozen pie stand at room
temperature for 5 minutes before slicing.

Tangerine Pie

Makes 1 (9-inch) pie

½ (14.1-ounce) package refrigerated
    pie crusts
1½ cups tangerine juice
½ cup sugar
2 tablespoons lime juice
¼ cup cornstarch
2 large eggs
2 tablespoons butter
2 cups heavy whipping cream*
½ cup confectioners' sugar*
Garnish: tangerine zest

1. Preheat oven to 450°. On a lightly
floured surface, roll dough into 11-inch
circle. Fit pie crust into a 9-inch pie
plate; fold edges under, and crimp.
Using a fork, prick bottom and sides of
pie crust. Bake for 10 minutes or until
golden brown. Cool completely on a
wire rack.

2. In a large saucepan, whisk
together tangerine juice, sugar, lime
juice, cornstarch, and eggs until
well combined. Bring to a boil over
medium heat, whisking constantly,
until thickened. Remove from heat,
and stir in butter. Pour mixture into a
stainless-steel bowl; place in a larger
bowl filled with ice, and chill to room
temperature, stirring often. Spoon
juice mixture into prepared crust.
Place heavy-duty plastic wrap directly
on custard (to prevent a film from
forming). Cover and chill for 8 hours or
until firm.

3. In a large bowl, beat cream until
soft peaks form. Add confectioners'
sugar, and beat until stiff peaks form.
Spoon whipped cream onto pie.
Garnish with tangerine zest, if desired.
Serve immediately.

*Frozen whipped topping may be used
in place of sweetened whipped cream.

Note: When making custard, do not
boil too long or the egg will curdle.
If egg begins to curdle, strain the
mixture through a fine-mesh sieve
into a bowl. Also, do not undercook or
the custard will not set up.

Festive Fête

REVEL IN MERRIMENT AND GLAD TIDINGS
THROUGHOUT THE HOLIDAYS BY HOSTING
FABULOUS PARTIES COMPLETE WITH TWISTS
ON TRADITIONAL CLASSICS. FROM GUMBO TO
BREAD PUDDING, THIS MENU IS SURE TO PLEASE.

On the Menu

SHRIMP AND ANDOUILLE GUMBO
BEEF TENDERLOIN WITH CREOLE MUSTARD SAUCE
RUSTIC MACARONI AND CHEESE   WHIPPED CAULIFLOWER
ZUCCHINI WITH LIMAS AND TOMATOES
BREAD PUDDING WITH PRALINE SAUCE

Shrimp and Andouille Gumbo

Makes 10 to 12 servings

8 tablespoons unsalted butter
½ cup all-purpose flour
½ cup chopped green bell pepper
½ cup chopped red bell pepper
½ cup chopped yellow onion
½ cup chopped celery
2 (14.5-ounce) cans diced tomatoes
1 tablespoon tomato paste
3 tablespoons Worcestershire sauce
10 cups chicken broth
2 tablespoons Cajun seasoning
1 pound frozen sliced okra
1 pound andouille sausage, cut into
    ½-inch pieces
1 pound peeled and deveined
    medium-large fresh shrimp
½ pound crabmeat, picked free of
    shell
Parsley Rice (recipe follows)

1. In a large stockpot or Dutch oven, melt butter over medium heat. Add flour, and cook, stirring constantly, for 20 minutes or until browned and fragrant. Add bell peppers, onion, and celery to flour mixture. Cook for 4 to 5 minutes or until onion begins to become translucent.

2. Add tomatoes, tomato paste, Worcestershire, chicken broth, and Cajun seasoning, stirring well. Bring to a boil; reduce heat to a simmer. Cook for 15 minutes, stirring often. Add okra and sausage. Cook for 5 to 6 minutes or until sausage is cooked through. Add shrimp and crabmeat, and cook just until shrimp are pink, stirring well. Remove from heat. Serve with Parsley Rice.

Parsley Rice

Makes 6 cups

4 cups water
2 cups uncooked long-grain white
    rice
4 tablespoons butter
¼ cup chopped fresh parsley
1 teaspoon salt

1. In a large saucepan, combine water and rice. Bring to a boil over medium-high heat; reduce heat to low. Cover and cook for 20 minutes or until rice is tender and liquid is absorbed. In a large bowl, combine rice, butter, parsley, and salt, fluffing with a fork.

Rustic Macaroni and Cheese

Makes 10 to 12 servings

6 tablespoons unsalted butter, divided
½ cup all-purpose flour
3 cups whole milk
8 ounces shredded mozzarella cheese
8 ounces shredded sharp Cheddar
    cheese
8 ounces shredded fontina cheese
1½ teaspoons salt, divided
1 teaspoon ground black pepper,
    divided
1 (16-ounce) box ziti pasta, cooked
    according to package directions
1 cup panko (Japanese bread crumbs)

1. Preheat oven to 350°. Spray a 3-quart baking dish with nonstick cooking spray.

2. In a large stockpot or Dutch oven, melt 4 tablespoons butter over medium heat. Add flour, whisking to combine. Cook for 2 to 3 minutes or until flour mixture is thickened, stirring constantly. Gradually add milk to flour mixture, whisking to remove any lumps. Cook for 3 to 5 minutes or until milk mixture begins to thicken, stirring often. Add cheeses, 1 teaspoon salt, and ½ teaspoon pepper, stirring well. Add prepared ziti to cheese mixture, stirring gently to coat. Spoon into prepared dish.

3. In a medium microwave-safe bowl, melt remaining 2 tablespoons butter. Add panko, remaining ½ teaspoon salt, and remaining ½ teaspoon pepper, stirring to combine. Spread over pasta. Bake for 30 minutes or until topping is golden brown.

of limas, and half of corn, stirring to combine. Add garlic and salt. Cook for 3 minutes, stirring occasionally. Place in a large bowl. Repeat with remaining half of ingredients, tossing gently.

Whipped Cauliflower
Makes about 8 servings

2 large heads cauliflower, stems and
   leaves removed
3 cups chicken broth
1 cup heavy whipping cream
4 tablespoons unsalted butter,
   softened
2 teaspoons salt
Olive oil
Garnish: fresh parsley

1. Preheat oven to 350°. Spray a 2-quart baking dish with nonstick cooking spray.

2. Cut cauliflower into 2-inch pieces. In a large stockpot or Dutch oven, combine cauliflower and chicken broth. Cover and bring to a boil over medium-high heat. Cook for 8 minutes or until cauliflower is tender. Drain.

3. In the work bowl of a food processor, pulse cauliflower, in batches if necessary, while gradually adding cream and butter until smooth. Add salt, and pulse to combine. Spoon into prepared dish. Bake for 20 minutes or until lightly golden on top. Drizzle with olive oil, and garnish with fresh parsley, if desired. Serve immediately.

Zucchini with Limas and Tomatoes
Makes 8 to 10 servings

2 cups frozen baby lima beans
1½ cups frozen corn kernels
½ cup extra-virgin olive oil, divided
4 medium zucchini, cut into 3½-inch
   pieces
2 pints cherry tomatoes, halved
2 cloves garlic, finely chopped
1 teaspoon salt

1. In a large microwave-safe dish, place lima beans and corn. Add ¼ inch water to bottom of dish. Cover and microwave on High for 1 minute or until limas are slightly tender. Drain.

2. In a large skillet, heat ¼ cup olive oil over medium-high heat. Add half of zucchini to pan. Cook for 2 to 3 minutes, stirring often, until crisp-tender. Add half of tomatoes, half

Beef Tenderloin with Creole Mustard Sauce

Makes 10 to 12 servings

1 (6-pound) beef tenderloin,
   trimmed
¼ cup extra-virgin olive oil
2 teaspoons Creole seasoning
1 teaspoon salt
1 teaspoon ground black pepper
Creole Mustard Sauce
   (recipe follows)
Garnish: fresh parsley and miniature
   bell peppers

1. Preheat oven to 400°. Line a rimmed baking sheet with aluminum foil.

2. Rub tenderloin with oil. Season with Creole seasoning, salt, and pepper, coating evenly. Bake for 35 to 45 minutes or until a meat thermometer inserted in the thickest part of the tenderloin registers 135° (rare). Let tenderloin stand for at least 15 minutes before slicing. Serve with Creole Mustard Sauce. Garnish with fresh parsley and miniature bell peppers, if desired.

Creole Mustard Sauce

Makes about 1 cup

4 tablespoons unsalted butter
3 large shallots, thinly sliced
3 tablespoons Creole mustard
1½ cups heavy whipping cream
Garnish: chopped fresh parsley

1. In a medium saucepan, melt butter over medium heat. Add shallot, and cook for 3 to 4 minutes or until translucent. Add mustard, stirring well. Add cream, whisking to remove any lumps. Reduce heat to medium-low. Cook for 7 to 10 minutes or until sauce is thickened, whisking frequently. Garnish with fresh parsley, if desired.

Tip: To keep meat tender and juicy, let it stand for 15 minutes after removing from the oven. This allows the juices to settle into the fibers in the meat and keeps it tender and moist. If you cut into the meat straight from oven, the juices will run out and the tenderloin will be dry.

Gather cherished ornaments, both old and new, and group together in the center of your table for a touching and personalized centerpiece.

Bread Pudding with Praline Sauce
Makes 10 to 12 servings

5 large eggs
¾ cup sugar
¾ cup firmly packed light brown sugar
2 cups heavy whipping cream
1 teaspoon vanilla extract
12 cups cubed French bread
1 cup diced Braeburn apple
1 cup raisins
½ cup chopped pecans
Praline Sauce (recipe follows)

1. Preheat oven to 350°.

2. In a large bowl, whisk eggs. Add sugars, cream, and vanilla, whisking until smooth. Add cubed bread to milk mixture. Chill for 1 hour or up to overnight.

3. Remove bread mixture from refrigerator, and let stand at room temperature for 30 minutes. Add diced apple, raisins, and pecans. Spray a 13x9-inch baking pan with nonstick baking spray with flour. Pour into prepared pan.

4. Bake for 1 hour or until a wooden pick inserted in the center comes out clean. Cover with aluminum foil if necessary to prevent excessive browning. Serve with Praline Sauce.

Praline Sauce
Makes about 1½ cups

½ cup unsalted butter
1 cup firmly packed light brown sugar
½ cup heavy whipping cream
½ cup toasted chopped pecans
1 teaspoon vanilla extract

1. In a medium saucepan, melt butter over medium heat. Add brown sugar and cream. Cook over medium heat, stirring constantly, for 3 to 4 minutes or until smooth. Add pecans and vanilla, stirring well. Serve warm.

Toasty Warm

WHEN THE CHILLY WINDS OF WINTER
BLOW, CURLING UP IN FRONT OF THE
FIREPLACE IS A PAMPERING PLEASURE
THAT'S IMPOSSIBLE TO RESIST.

CREAMY HERBED SPINACH SOUP

HAM AND JARLSBERG SANDWICHES AND
ROAST BEEF ROLL-UPS WITH MAYTAG BLUE
CHEESE AND CARAMELIZED ONIONS

On the Menu

CREAMY HERBED SPINACH SOUP

HAM AND JARLSBERG SANDWICHES

ROAST BEEF ROLL-UPS WITH MAYTAG BLUE CHEESE AND
CARAMELIZED ONIONS

GINGERBREAD FINGERS WITH ORANGE CRÈME FILLING

DARK CHOCOLATE RASPBERRY MOUSSE CAKE

Creamy Herbed Spinach Soup

Makes 5 cups

2 tablespoons olive oil
1 small onion, chopped
2 cloves garlic, minced
2 cups chicken broth
2 (6-ounce) packages fresh baby
 spinach
2 tablespoons chopped fresh basil
2 tablespoons chopped fresh parsley
1 cup heavy cream
½ cup sour cream
⅓ cup grated Parmesan cheese
½ teaspoon salt
½ teaspoon ground black pepper
Garnish: croutons and shredded
 Parmesan cheese

1. In Dutch oven over medium-high heat, heat olive oil. Sauté onion until tender; add garlic, and sauté 1 to 2 minutes.

2. Add chicken broth and spinach. Bring to boil; reduce heat, cover, and simmer for 10 minutes, stirring occasionally.

3. Add basil and parsley; purée with an immersion blender or process in batches in the container of a blender. Return to heat, and add cream and sour cream; simmer for 1 minute.

4. Add Parmesan cheese, salt, and pepper, stirring until cheese melts. Garnish with croutons and shredded Parmesan cheese, if desired.

Ham and Jarlsberg Sandwiches

Makes 6 sandwiches

¼ cup mayonnaise
2 tablespoons honey mustard
Parmesan Rosemary Bread
 (recipe follows)
6 thin slices Virginia ham
6 thin slices Jarlsberg cheese

1. In a small bowl, combine mayonnaise and honey mustard. Slice bread into ½-inch slices.

2. Using a 2-inch square cutter, cut out 12 squares of bread. Spread mayonnaise mixture evenly over one side of each bread slice. Top six slices with ham and cheese. Top with remaining prepared bread over cheese.

Parmesan Rosemary Bread

Makes 1 loaf

2½ cups all-purpose flour
⅓ cup grated Parmesan cheese
1 tablespoon sugar
1 tablespoon chopped fresh
 rosemary
2 teaspoons dried minced onion
1 teaspoon baking soda
½ teaspoon salt
1 cup sour cream
⅓ cup milk
¼ cup butter, melted

1. Preheat oven to 350°. Spray a 9x5-inch loaf pan with nonstick baking spray with flour.

2. In a large bowl, combine flour, cheese, sugar, rosemary, onion, baking soda, and salt. Add sour cream, milk, and butter. Beat at medium speed with a mixer until well combined.

3. Place dough in prepared loaf pan. Bake for 35 to 40 minutes or until a wooden pick inserted in center comes out clean.

4. Cool in pan for 10 minutes. Remove from pan, and cool completely on a wire rack.

Roast Beef Roll-ups with Maytag Blue Cheese and Caramelized Onions

Makes 12 roll-ups

¾ cup Maytag blue cheese,
 crumbled
¼ cup mayonnaise
2 tablespoons sour cream
½ teaspoon cracked black pepper
2 burrito-size sun-dried tomato
 tortillas
2 burrito-size spinach tortillas
½ pound thinly sliced deli roast
 beef
Caramelized Onions (recipe follows)

1. In small bowl, combine blue cheese, mayonnaise, sour cream, and pepper.

2. Spread mixture evenly on tortillas, leaving a ½-inch border. Evenly layer

roast beef and Caramelized Onions on top of blue cheese mixture.

3. Roll up each tortilla; place seam side down on a serving platter. Trim ¼ inch off each end, and slice into thirds. Serve immediately.

Caramelized Onions
Makes 1 cup

¼ cup butter
1½ pounds onions, sliced ⅛ inch thick
3 tablespoons balsamic vinegar
½ teaspoon salt
¼ teaspoon ground black pepper

1. In large saucepan over medium-low heat, melt butter.

2. Add onions; cover and cook for 30 minutes, stirring occasionally. Uncover and increase heat to medium-high. Cook onions, stirring frequently, until caramelized, about 20 minutes.

3. Add vinegar, salt, and pepper, and stir until vinegar evaporates, 1 to 2 minutes.

Gingerbread Fingers with Orange Crème Filling
Makes 10 fingers

1½ cups all-purpose flour
½ cup sugar
1 teaspoon baking soda
1 teaspoon ground ginger
½ teaspoon ground cinnamon
½ cup water
⅓ cup dark molasses
¼ cup butter, melted
1 large egg
½ teaspoon vanilla extract
Orange Crème Filling
  (recipe follows)
Garnish: orange zest and orange
  slices

1. Preheat oven to 350°. Spray a 9-inch square pan with nonstick baking spray with flour.

2. In a medium bowl, combine flour, sugar, baking soda, ginger, and cinnamon.

3. In a large bowl, combine water, molasses, butter, egg, and vanilla; beat at medium speed with a mixer until smooth.

4. Add flour mixture to molasses mixture, beating well. Pour batter into prepared pan.

5. Bake for 25 to 30 minutes or until wooden pick inserted in center comes out clean. Cool in pan on a wire rack for 10 minutes. Remove from pan, and cool completely on wire rack.

6. With a serrated knife, trim ¾ inch from each side of gingerbread; cut into about 4x1½-inch fingers.

7. Cut each finger in half horizontally, and evenly spread Orange Crème Filling on bottom half of gingerbread fingers; replace tops. Garnish with orange crème, orange zest, and orange slices, if desired.

Orange Crème Filling
Makes 1 cup

1 (3-ounce) package cream cheese, softened
¼ cup butter, softened
1 teaspoon orange zest
1 cup confectioners' sugar

1. In a medium bowl, combine cream cheese, butter, and orange zest; beat at medium speed with a mixer until smooth. Add confectioners' sugar, and beat until smooth.

Teatime by the fire is an ideal indulgence during the Christmas season. The perfect accompaniment? Decadent chocolate cake!

Dark Chocolate Raspberry Mousse Cake
Makes 1 (6-inch) cake

2 cups sugar
½ cup butter, softened
2 large eggs
2 cups all-purpose flour
2 teaspoons baking soda
½ teaspoon salt
½ cup buttermilk
⅓ cup unsweetened dark cocoa
    powder
2 tablespoons vegetable oil
1 teaspoon vanilla extract
1 cup boiling water
Raspberry Mousse (recipe follows)
Chocolate Ganache Icing
    (recipe follows)
Garnish: fresh raspberries and edible
    flowers

1. Preheat oven to 350°. Spray 3 (6x2-inch) cake pans with nonstick baking spray with flour.

2. In a large bowl, beat sugar and butter at medium speed with a mixer until fluffy. Add eggs, one at a time, beating well after each addition.

3. In a medium bowl, combine flour, baking soda, and salt. In another medium bowl, combine buttermilk, cocoa powder, oil, and vanilla. Add flour mixture to butter mixture alternately with buttermilk mixture, beginning and ending with flour mixture. Add boiling water, and beat at medium speed until blended.

4. Pour batter into prepared pans. Bake for 40 to 45 minutes or until a wooden pick inserted in center comes out clean. Cool in pans on wire racks for 10 minutes. Remove cakes from pans, and cool completely on wire racks.

5. To assemble, place one cake layer on a serving plate; spread half of Raspberry Mousse on top of cake layer; top with another cake layer; repeat with remaining Raspberry Mousse. Top with remaining cake layer. Pour chocolate ganache over center of cake, allowing excess to cover sides. Garnish with fresh raspberries and edible flowers, if desired.

Raspberry Mousse
Makes about 2 cups

2 tablespoons cold water
1 teaspoon unflavored gelatin
½ cup frozen raspberries, thawed
1 tablespoon lemon juice
½ cup sugar
1 tablespoon raspberry liqueur
½ cup heavy cream

1. In small microwave-safe bowl, combine water and gelatin; let stand for 5 minutes. Microwave on High, for 1 minute, stirring until gelatin dissolves.

2. In the container of a blender, purée raspberries and lemon juice; strain, discarding seeds.

3. In a medium saucepan, combine raspberry purée and sugar over medium heat. Cook, stirring occasionally, until sugar dissolves, about 5 minutes. Stir in raspberry liqueur and dissolved gelatin.

4. Remove from heat, and chill raspberry mixture for 2 hours.

5. In a medium bowl, beat cream at high speed with a mixer until stiff peaks form. Add raspberry mixture, beating at low speed just until combined; chill for 2 hours.

Chocolate Ganache Icing
Makes about 2 cups

1¼ cups heavy cream
¼ cup sugar
¼ cup corn syrup
1½ cups semisweet chocolate
    morsels

1. In medium saucepan over medium heat, combine cream, sugar, and corn syrup, stirring until sugar dissolves. Stir in chocolate until melted and smooth. Cool slightly before using.

Come Visit and
DINE

From ornament swaps to elegant soirées,
yuletide festivities are ideal for serving a variety
of enticing hors d'oeuvres. Small in size yet
full in flavor, these showstopping savories are
guaranteed crowd-pleasers.

ROAST BEEF FINGER SANDWICHES WITH
KALAMATA MUSTARD BUTTER

Tiny Appetizers

KEEP THE OFFERINGS ON THE SMALL SIDE FOR HOLIDAY COMPANY.
FROM A BITE-SIZE SCONE TO A PETITE SHRIMP CUP, THESE
DELICIOUS RECIPES WILL DELIGHT YOUR FRIENDS AND FAMILY.

On the Menu

Shrimp Mousse with Saffron Aïoli in Phyllo Cups
Roast Beef Finger Sandwiches with
Kalamata Mustard Butter
Honey Scones with Apricot Preserves
Brandy Cream in Chocolate Cups
Lemon-glazed Miniature Cakes

SHRIMP MOUSSE WITH SAFFRON
AÏOLI IN PHYLLO CUPS

BRANDY CREAM IN CHOCOLATE CUPS AND
LEMON-GLAZED MINIATURE CAKES

Lemon-glazed Miniature Cakes

Makes 36 tea cakes

1 cup butter
1¾ cups sugar
2 large eggs
1 teaspoon vanilla extract
3½ cups all-purpose flour
1 teaspoon baking soda
1 teaspoon cream of tartar
¾ cup plus 2 tablespoons
   buttermilk
¾ cup plus 2 tablespoons
   confectioners' sugar
2 tablespoons fresh lemon juice
Garnish: whipped cream and lemon
   zest

1. Preheat oven to 350°. Spray mini muffin pans with nonstick cooking spray.

2. In a large bowl, beat butter and sugar at medium-high speed with a mixer until fluffy. Add eggs, one at a time, beating well after each addition. Stir in vanilla.

3. In a medium bowl, combine flour, baking soda, and cream of tartar. Add to butter mixture alternately with buttermilk, beginning and ending with flour mixture.

4. Spoon batter into mini muffin pans, filling three-fourths full. Bake for 15 to 18 minutes or until a wooden pick inserted in center comes out clean. Cool in pans for 2 minutes. Remove tea cakes from pans, and cool completely on wire racks.

5. In a small bowl, combine confectioners' sugar and lemon juice, stirring until smooth. Brush cooled tea cakes with lemon glaze. Garnish with whipped cream and lemon zest, if desired.

Roast Beef Finger Sandwiches with Kalamata Mustard Butter

Makes 15 sandwiches

½ cup butter, softened
½ cup chopped kalamata olives
¼ cup deli-style mustard
1 tablespoon chopped fresh parsley
⅛ teaspoon ground black pepper
5 slices wheat bread, crusts
   removed
5 slices white bread, crusts
   removed
¼ pound thinly sliced deli roast beef
Garnish: blanched chives, fresh
   parsley, and pimiento

1. In the work bowl of a food processor, pulse butter, olives, mustard, parsley, and pepper until combined but still chunky.

2. Spread butter mixture on wheat bread slices; top white bread slices with thinly sliced roast beef. Place remaining bread slices on top of roast beef.

3. Cut sandwiches into fingers. Garnish by wrapping each with a blanched chive, and tie in knot. Trim ends of chives, if necessary. Tuck fresh parsley in center of tie, and top with pimiento, if desired.

Shrimp Mousse with Saffron Aïoli in Phyllo Cups

Makes 30 shells

½ pound large fresh shrimp, cooked
1 (8-ounce) package cream cheese,
   softened
½ cup butter, softened
1 clove garlic, minced
1 tablespoon minced fresh chives
2 (2.1-ounce) packages frozen mini-
   phyllo pastry shells, thawed
Saffron Aïoli (recipe follows)
Garnish: baby shrimp and chopped
   fresh parsley

1. Peel and devein large shrimp.

2. In the work bowl of a food processor, add cream cheese, butter, garlic, and chives; process until combined. Add large shrimp, and pulse until shrimp are coarsely chopped.

3. Spoon mixture into phyllo shells. Drizzle with Saffron Aïoli. Garnish with baby shrimp and parsley, if desired.

Saffron Aïoli

Makes about ½ cup

½ cup mayonnaise
2 tablespoons heavy cream
½ teaspoon Dijon mustard
Pinch of saffron
1 clove garlic, minced

1. In a small bowl, combine mayonnaise, cream, mustard, saffron, and garlic until well blended.

Chocolate-dipped Apricots

Chocolate-dipped apricots are easy to prepare and make delicious little additions to your Christmas table. To prepare: Dip dried apricot halves halfway into melted chocolate-flavored candy coating, allowing excess to drip off. Place on a wax paper-lined pan, and chill for one hour. For more Christmas spirit, add a tablespoon of brandy to the candy coating. Leave out the brandy to keep these kid-friendly.

Honey Scones with Apricot Preserves

Makes 15 scones

2¼ cups all-purpose flour
¼ cup sugar
2½ teaspoons baking powder
¾ teaspoon ground ginger
¼ teaspoon salt
½ cup butter
¼ cup honey
½ cup plus 1 tablespoon heavy cream
Sparkling sugar

1. Preheat oven to 350°. Spray a baking sheet with nonstick cooking spray.

2. In a large bowl, combine flour, sugar, baking powder, ginger, and salt. Using a pastry blender, cut in butter until mixture is crumbly.

3. In a small bowl, combine honey and ½ cup cream. Add to dry ingredients, stirring just until moistened.

4. On lightly floured surface, roll dough to ½-inch thickness. Using a 3-inch cutter, cut out scones, and place on prepared baking sheet. Reroll dough scraps, and cut out until all dough is used. Brush with remaining 1 tablespoon cream, and sprinkle with sparkling sugar. Bake for 18 to 20 minutes or until lightly browned. Serve with Apricot Preserves.

Apricot Preserves

Makes 4½ cups

3 cups finely chopped dried apricots
3 cups water
2 cups sugar

1. In a 3-quart slow cooker, combine apricots, water, and sugar.

2. Cook, covered, on High for 3½ hours, stirring occasionally.

3. Uncover and cook 1 hour longer, stirring occasionally. Cover and chill.

Brandy Cream in Chocolate Cups

Makes 36 cordial cups

2 cups heavy cream
½ cup confectioners' sugar
3 tablespoons brandy
3 (3.15-ounce) boxes molded
    chocolate cordial cups
Sugared Almonds (recipe follows)
Thinly sliced strawberries

1. In a medium bowl, beat cream at medium speed with a mixer until soft peaks form.

2. Add confectioners' sugar, 1 tablespoon at a time, beating until stiff peaks form. Stir in brandy.

3. Spoon brandy cream into chocolate cordial cups. Sprinkle with Sugared Almonds, and place each cup on strawberry slice.

Sugared Almonds

Makes about ½ cup

2 tablespoons butter
½ cup sliced almonds
2 tablespoons sugar

1. In small skillet, melt butter over medium heat.

2. Stir in almonds, and cook until lightly browned, stirring frequently. Add sugar, stirring to coat. Spoon mixture onto wax paper to cool.

Ornament Swap Party

ADDING A TOUCH OF SPARKLE AND CHARACTER TO YOUR CHRISTMAS TREE WITH FAMILIAR KEEPSAKES AND NEW TOUCHES IS AN EASY WAY TO SPREAD CHEER. THAT'S WHY ORNAMENT SWAPS ARE ALWAYS A BIG HIT—ESPECIALLY WHEN DELICIOUS TREATS AND SNACKS ARE SERVED DURING THE FESTIVITIES.

AMARETTO CHEESECAKE SQUARES,
KAHÚLA AND COFFEE FUDGE, AND
PECAN PIE TARTLETS

PROSCIUTTO AND BRIE DIP

On the Menu

PROSCIUTTO AND BRIE DIP
MINI POTATO SKINS WITH HORSERADISH DIPPING SAUCE
PIZZA ROLLS WITH MARINARA SAUCE   PECAN PIE TARTLETS
KAHLÚA AND COFFEE FUDGE
AMARETTO CHEESECAKE SQUARES   HOT RUM PUNCH

Mini Potato Skins with Horseradish Dipping Sauce

Makes 24 skins

12 small red potatoes
3 tablespoons olive oil, divided
1 teaspoon Creole seasoning
½ teaspoon salt
¼ teaspoon ground black pepper
1½ cups shredded Cheddar and Monterey Jack cheese blend
8 slices bacon, cooked and crumbled
¼ cup chopped green onion
Horseradish Dipping Sauce (recipe follows)

1. Preheat oven to 375°. Line a baking sheet with aluminum foil. Rub potatoes with 1 tablespoon olive oil to coat skins. Place on prepared baking sheet. Bake for 45 minutes or until tender. Set aside potatoes until cool enough to handle.

2. Cut potatoes in half; using a teaspoon or melon baller, scoop out pulp, leaving ¼-inch-thick shells. Reserve potato pulp for another use.

3. In a small bowl, combine remaining 2 tablespoons olive oil, Creole seasoning, salt, and pepper.

Brush inside of potatoes with olive oil mixture. Bake for 15 minutes. Top with cheese, bacon, and green onion; bake for 5 minutes or until cheese is melted. Serve with Horseradish Dipping Sauce.

Horseradish Dipping Sauce

Makes 1½ cups

1 cup sour cream
½ cup mayonnaise
2 tablespoons prepared horseradish
1 tablespoon chopped fresh chives
¼ teaspoon salt
¼ teaspoon ground black pepper

1. In a small bowl, combine sour cream, mayonnaise, horseradish, chives, salt, and pepper. Cover and chill until ready to serve.

Prosciutto and Brie Dip

Makes 10 to 12 servings

1 cup sour cream
1 (8-ounce) package cream cheese, softened
3 (5-ounce) containers crème de Brie*
½ cup grated Parmesan cheese
1½ cups chopped prosciutto (about 6 ounces)
¼ cup chopped green onion
½ teaspoon crushed red pepper
Garnish: chopped green onion

1. Preheat oven to 375°. In a large bowl, combine sour cream, cream cheese, crème de Brie, and Parmesan cheese. Beat at medium speed with a mixer until smooth. Add prosciutto, green onion, and red pepper, beating to combine. Spoon mixture into an 8-inch square baking dish. Bake for 15 to 20 minutes or until bubbly. Transfer to a serving dish. Serve with crackers or Melba toast rounds, and garnish with chopped green onion, if desired.

97

Kahlúa and Coffee Fudge
Makes 10 to 12 servings

1 (14-ounce) can sweetened
   condensed milk
¼ cup Kahlúa
2 tablespoons instant coffee
   granules
1 (12-ounce) package semisweet
   chocolate morsels
1 cup chopped pecans
½ teaspoon vanilla extract

1. Line an 8-inch square baking pan
with aluminum foil, allowing foil to
extend several inches over edges of
pan. In a large heavy-duty saucepan,
combine condensed milk, Kahlúa, and
coffee granules over medium heat.
Bring to a simmer; cook for 2 minutes,
stirring constantly, until mixture thickens
slightly. Remove from heat, and stir in
chocolate morsels until melted and
smooth. Stir in pecans and vanilla.

2. Spread evenly into prepared pan.
Chill for 2 hours. Remove fudge from
pan using foil as handles. Remove foil,
and cut into squares.

Amaretto Cheesecake Squares
Makes 24 squares

1¾ cups all-purpose flour, divided
½ cup firmly packed light brown sugar
½ cup butter, melted
2 (8-ounce) packages cream cheese, softened
½ cup sugar
4 large eggs
¼ cup amaretto liqueur
½ teaspoon almond extract
⅓ cup sliced almonds

1. Preheat oven to 350°. Combine 1½ cups flour, brown sugar, and melted butter. Press firmly into bottom of a 13x9-inch baking pan. Bake for 6 to 8 minutes.

2. In a large bowl, combine cream cheese, sugar, and remaining ¼ cup flour. Beat at medium speed with a mixer until well combined. Add eggs, one at a time, beating well after each addition. Add amaretto and almond extract, beating to combine.

3. Spread filling over prepared crust; sprinkle with sliced almonds. Bake for 25 minutes or until set. Cool completely. Cover, and chill for 2 hours or overnight. Cut into squares.

Pizza Rolls with Marinara Sauce

Makes 12 rolls

2 tablespoons olive oil
1 cup chopped fresh mushrooms
½ cup chopped onion
¼ cup chopped red bell pepper
½ teaspoon salt
¼ teaspoon ground black pepper
6 cloves garlic, minced
½ pound ground Italian sausage,
　　cooked and crumbled
1 cup chopped pepperoni
1 (12-ounce) can tomato paste
1 cup shredded Italian three-cheese
　　blend
12 egg roll wrappers
1 large egg, lightly beaten
Vegetable oil
Marinara Sauce (recipe follows)

1. In a large sauté pan, heat olive oil over medium heat. Add mushrooms, onion, red pepper, salt, and pepper. Cook for 4 to 5 minutes or until vegetables are tender. Add garlic, and cook 1 minute. Add sausage, pepperoni, and tomato paste, stirring to mix well. Cook 2 to 3 minutes, stirring constantly. Remove from heat, drain, and cool slightly; stir in cheese.

2. Spoon 2 tablespoons filling on bottom one-third of egg roll wrapper. Fold the lower corner over filling, and roll up about one-third of the way. Brush the left and right corners of wrapper with beaten egg; fold corners toward center of filling. Brush top edge with egg, and roll up tightly; repeat with remaining egg roll wrappers, filling, and beaten egg.

3. In a Dutch oven, pour oil to a depth of 2 inches; heat to 350°. Fry pizza rolls, in batches, 3 to 4 minutes or until golden brown. Drain on paper towels. Serve immediately with Marinara Sauce.

Marinara Sauce

Makes 2½ cups

1 tablespoon olive oil
3 cloves garlic, minced
1 (28-ounce) can crushed
　　tomatoes
1 tablespoon Italian seasoning
1 teaspoon sugar
½ teaspoon salt
¼ teaspoon ground black
　　pepper

1. In a medium saucepan, heat olive oil over medium heat. Add garlic, and cook for 1 minute. Add tomatoes, Italian seasoning, sugar, salt, and pepper, stirring to combine. Reduce heat to low, and simmer, uncovered, for 20 minutes. Serve warm.

Pecan Pie Tartlets

Makes 36 tartlets

Crust:
½ cup sugar
¼ cup butter, softened
1 (3-ounce) package cream cheese, softened
1 large egg
1¾ cups all-purpose flour

Filling:
⅓ cup light corn syrup
⅓ cup dark corn syrup
½ cup sugar
2 tablespoons butter, melted
2 large eggs, lightly beaten
1 teaspoon vanilla extract
¾ cup finely chopped pecans

1. To prepare crust: In a medium bowl, combine sugar, butter, and cream cheese. Beat at medium speed with a mixer until fluffy. Add egg, beating until smooth. Gradually add flour. Beat at low speed until just combined (dough will be sticky). Cover and chill dough for 1 hour.

2. Preheat oven to 350°. Roll dough into 1-inch balls; press in bottom and two-thirds up sides of each cup of 3 (12-cup) miniature muffin pans.

3. To prepare filling: In a medium bowl, combine corn syrups, sugar, melted butter, eggs, and vanilla, whisking to combine. Spoon corn syrup mixture into each prepared crust. Top with chopped pecans. Bake for 18 to 20 minutes or until lightly browned.

Hot Rum Punch

Makes about 3 quarts

1 (64-ounce) bottle apple cider
½ cup sugar
3 cinnamon sticks
1 tablespoon whole cloves
2 cups fresh orange juice
1 cup light rum
½ cup fresh lemon juice
Garnish: fresh orange slices and whole cloves

1. In a Dutch oven over medium heat, combine apple cider, sugar, cinnamon sticks, and cloves. Simmer, uncovered, for 10 minutes; remove and discard spices. Add orange juice, rum, and lemon juice, and heat mixture thoroughly. Garnish with fresh orange slices studded with cloves, if desired.

A Savory Start

DELICIOUS APPETIZERS ARE THE PERFECT
START TO ANY HOLIDAY PARTY OR GATHERING.

On the Menu

Black-eyed Pea Salsa
Bacon-wrapped Breadsticks
Sausage Wontons   Cumin Pita Chips
Cranberries and Brie Wrapped in Phyllo
with Gingersnaps and Green Apple Slices

Black-eyed Pea Salsa
Makes 6 cups

3 (15.8-ounce) cans black-eyed peas,
    drained and rinsed
1 (10-ounce) can diced tomatoes
    with green chiles
1 small onion, finely chopped
1 jalapeño pepper, seeded and
    minced
2 cloves garlic, minced
1 cup chopped fresh cilantro
1 teaspoon salt
½ teaspoon ground black pepper
1 tablespoon olive oil
Cumin Pita Chips (recipe follows)

1. In a large bowl, combine black-eyed peas, tomatoes, onion, jalapeño, garlic, cilantro, salt, and pepper. Add olive oil, and toss gently. Serve with Cumin Pita Chips.

Cumin Pita Chips
Makes 48 chips

3 (6-inch) pita bread rounds, split
¼ cup butter, melted
2 teaspoons garlic salt
2 teaspoons ground cumin

1. Preheat oven to 350°. Cut each bread half into 8 wedges.

2. Place wedges in a single layer on an ungreased baking sheet. Brush wedges with melted butter, and sprinkle evenly with garlic salt and cumin.

3. Bake for 6 to 8 minutes or until lightly browned.

Cranberries and Brie Wrapped in Phyllo

Makes 1 Brie

1 (35.2-ounce) round Brie cheese
12 frozen phyllo pastry sheets,
  thawed
½ cup butter, melted and divided
1 cup whole-berry cranberry sauce
1 tablespoon brown sugar
¼ cup chopped pecans
Gingersnaps and green apple slices

1. Preheat oven to 425°. Line a large baking sheet with heavy-duty aluminum foil.

2. Trim rind from top of Brie, discarding rind; set cheese aside.

3. Place 2 sheets of phyllo on foil, overlapping to make a 14-inch square. (Keep remaining phyllo covered with a clean damp kitchen towel to prevent drying out.) Brush phyllo with melted butter. Repeat procedure with remaining phyllo (2 sheets at a time) and butter, reserving ¼ cup butter.

3. Place Brie in center of phyllo. Make shallow indentations in top of Brie with a fork at ½-inch intervals. Pour remaining ¼ cup butter over Brie.

4. Spread cranberry sauce over top of Brie. Sprinkle with brown sugar and pecans.

5. Fold phyllo up over edges of Brie, and crimp edges of dough with hands. Fold foil lightly around edges of Brie to hold phyllo in place while baking.

6. Bake for 10 to 15 minutes or until phyllo is lightly browned. Let cool for 20 minutes. Remove foil. Serve with gingersnaps and green apple slices.

Sausage Wontons

Makes 60 wontons

1 pound ground pork sausage
1 (8-ounce) package cream cheese,
  softened
4 green onions, diced
⅛ teaspoon ground red pepper
60 wonton wrappers
Vegetable oil

1. In a large skillet, cook sausage over medium heat until browned and crumbly. Drain well.

2. In a small bowl, combine cooked sausage, cream cheese, green onions, and ground red pepper.

3. Place 1 teaspoon sausage mixture in center of each wonton wrapper. Moisten wonton wrapper edges with water. Bring corners together, pressing to seal.

4. In a Dutch oven, pour oil to a depth of 2 inches, and heat to 350°. Fry wontons in batches until golden, turning once. Drain on paper towels. Serve immediately with prepared salsa.

Bacon-wrapped Breadsticks

Makes about 36 breadsticks

¾ cup lightly packed brown sugar
3 tablespoons chili powder
1 (16-ounce) package thin-sliced
  bacon
1 (3-ounce) package thin
  breadsticks*

1. Preheat oven to 350°. Line a 15x10-inch jelly-roll pan with aluminum foil.

2. In a pie plate, combine brown sugar and chili powder; set aside.

3. Cut bacon in half lengthwise. Wrap 1 piece of bacon around each breadstick. Roll each breadstick in brown sugar mixture. Place breadsticks in a single layer on a wire rack. Place rack in prepared pan.

4. Bake for 20 to 25 minutes. Let cool for 10 to 15 minutes. Serve at room temperature.

*Look for these breadsticks in the gourmet cracker or Italian food section of the grocery store.

Joyful Christmas STYLE

For many, decorating our home's halls and hearths is the most beloved ritual of the holiday season. Poring over new ideas for inspiration keeps our daydreams full for months, as each new year offers a blank canvas for custom creations.

A Natural Noël

FRESH GREENERY, FRUIT, AND FLOWERS GO A LONG
WAY IN SPRUCING UP YOUR HOME FOR THE HOLIDAYS.

Simple Style

A creamy white dining room can be the perfect canvas for a calm and bright winter. There's no need to embellish the space with over-the-top holiday displays; rather, let natural elements work their wonder, and stick with the ease and simplicity of fresh blooms and greenery.

A holly, jolly home needn't be bedecked in Christmas baubles. Create classic charm with fresh greenery, fruit, and flowers throughout the house. For the finest in sensory delight, select live garland to frame sunny windows and stately hearths. The pop of natural color is especially pleasing in a cozy, neutral-palette space. From your wreaths to your tables, whether pine, fir, or cedar, lush greenery offers the scent of the season all through the holidays.

Left, Get in the giving spirit with these beautiful bundles of baked goods. Wrap homemade goodies in white paper or cheesecloth, and tie them with simple twine and twigs.

Tied Up
Bow-tied pinecone
swags add height
to this sun-soaked
porch's holiday décor,
accenting the room's
glorious windows with
extra emphasis on
nature's offerings.

Mother Nature's bounty can be integrated in magnificent mantels. Bring the beauty inside by layering festive fruits, such as citrus or pear, with lush leaves and boughs. Finally, a pretty pot of delicate, fragrant paperwhites accents your décor with subtle serenity.

Bring on the green! Inspired by tradition, tuck sprigs of fresh fir throughout to create seasonal splendor. And don't feel bound to berries—add a plump pineapple, the symbol of hospitality, to complete a fresh centerpiece.

All A-board

Instead of tucking wooden cutting boards away in the cupboard, create an eye-catching display by arranging them in alternating patterns. Need more boards? What a wonderful excuse to visit your favorite antiques shop!

A Nod to Nostalgia

CAPTURE THE WONDER OF THE HOLIDAY SEASON BY
PUTTING TIMELESS TREASURES IN A PLACE OF HONOR.

Twinkle Twinkle
Who can deny the beauty of a
silver and gold scene? Create
a striking tablescape with this
sparkling palette.

Fancy Feet

Shine a spotlight on holiday memories of yore. Do fanciful figure-eights on ice remind you of wonderful winters? Then add a prized pair of skates to a grapevine wreath. Other ideas include ballet slippers reminiscent of evenings at *The Nutcracker* or even handmade booties marking baby's first Christmas.

For many, much of the magic of this festive time of year is wrapped up in the joy of collecting. As we bring each box marked "Christmas" down from the attic, we take great care in unwrapping the enchantment cradled inside. From fragile figurines to antique ornaments, these cherished treasures of Christmases past handed down from generation to generation fill our hearts and homes with the joy and spirit of the season.

Heirloom laces and linens become the perfect palette for a snow-white scene, while mirrors on a mantel reflect twinkling silvers and golds in a vignette of tiny trees. On the table, a gilded snowflake accents your plate, while reindeer, snowmen, and angels offer a joyful centerpiece. From there, a charming tabletop scene is sure to delight when guests spot the village full of Jolly Old St. Nicks. With this holiday dazzler, you're guaranteed that wee boys and girls will be certain to select their favorite Kris Kringle, and maybe even whisper a Christmas wish in his ear.

On That Note

Friends and family fill your mailbox with lovely cards and letters each season. Don't simply toss aside these easy pieces of art— frame your favorite cards to keep a loved one's sweet sentiment alive from year to year.

A Classic Christmas

A RICH RED- AND GREEN-INSPIRED
THEME SERVES AS THE CENTERPIECE FOR
THIS RUSTICALLY ELEGANT HAVEN.

B oasting quite a collection of fine furniture and delicate dinnerware, these homeowners strike a harmonious chord when it comes to creating easy holiday elegance. Take, for instance, the colorful and inviting den, where guests are welcome to cozy up by the fire or select a seat at the table by the mint green buffet.

Have yourself a cup of cheer and enjoy the understated elegance of a tray of glass decanters accented with red berries. Other accessories, such as pretty tea towels and festive pillows, can be layered atop everyday solid patterns, adding easy whimsy to the room.

Bursting with brilliance, a colorful tree showcases the family's favorite decorations, while a selection of solid ornaments dangles from doorways and lights like mistletoe.

These homeowners know it's easy to get carried away with the classic colors of Christmas. But look beyond red and green—think forest and lime, cherry and scarlet—to add new life to a classic holiday palette.

Delicate Details
A vast collection of treasured china comes in handy for mixing, matching, and even decorating with holiday hues.

A Simpler Season

THIS HUMBLE HOMEOWNER
PREFERS A MORE LAID BACK
AND SENTIMENTAL YULETIDE.

The homeowner painted the brick above this mantle a very pale blue. After a good bit of dabbing, she achieved this fresh whitewashed look reminiscent of a cozy cottage.

Christmas cheer comes in many different packages. For this former antiques store owner, a symbolic season needn't be filled with over-the-top decorations in glittering silver and gold. Rather, a pared-down selection of prized possessions seems to suit this family perfectly.

Take, for instance, their beloved tree tradition. "We have a tiny little cottage without much room for a big Christmas tree," the homeowner explains. "My husband and I love to go out and pick a perfectly modest one right from the woods." A few strands of lights and her mother's vintage ornaments and soon the glowing display draws plenty of awe.

By the fire, an equally easy setup is sure to delight. Framed floral prints become particularly festive when flanked by a trio of tiny topiaries. Gracing the mantel, fresh greenery, lights, and pinecones are tucked into permanent garland to create an aromatic strand of simple Christmas cheer.

Editing her collection to include only the most precious decorations adds character and meaning—ideal for a smaller space, especially during the holidays when family and friends fill homes to the brim.

A Tisket, a Tasket
"I'm mad about red, and I love old plaids," the homeowner reveals, "so these old picnic baskets offer great festive storage adjacent to our tree." *Right,* A wonderful reminder of the reason for the season, this antique nativity passed down through generations takes its place of honor amid heirloom china.

Warmest Wishes

FROM SCENTED CANDLES AND
TWINKLE LIGHTS TO WARMING
THROWS AND ROARING
FIREPLACES, THIS HOME OFFERS
GUESTS A COZY WELCOME.

Clever Collecting

Holiday-themed collections needn't seem kitschy. In fact, they can be fun! Here, delightful deer, moose, and other wondrous wildlife bask in the warmth of the wood-burning fire.

The holidays are all about loved ones, says this homeowner, and what better way to show you care than opening up your cozy abode to welcome friends and family for a stay? Arriving through a charming front gate, visitors are greeted by twinkling tree topiaries and bow-bedecked sconces as they enter this enchanting holiday house. Inside, they delight in the attention to detail—every surface sings of the joy of the season.

After feasting on a delicious dinner served at a holiday-ready table, they'll move to the keeping room to sip a mug of steamy hot cocoa by one of the family's three fireplaces. As they drift from room to room, eyes will play "I Spy" with the homeowner's beloved Santa Clauses, which increase in number year after year. These days, grandchildren ages 6 to 16 arrange the keepsake collection at the family's Thanksgiving gathering, continuing a joyful tradition from generation to generation.

Want guests to linger long after dessert? Offer plenty of seating on a pretty porch. If yuletide carolers come to call, guests will have front-row seats for the spirited show.

Warm Welcome

The symmetry of wreaths, trees, topiaries, and sconces creates
subtle stylish curb appeal that's sure to delight guests all season.

304

Merry & Bright

WHEN GUESTS COME CALLING THIS WINTER,
WELCOME THEM INTO A HAPPY HOME BURSTING
WITH CHRISTMAS JOY. SEARCH THE ATTIC—
OR YOUR FAVORITE ANTIQUES SHOP—FOR
COLORFUL FINDS, AND DELIGHT IN THE
EXCITEMENT OF DECORATING OUTSIDE THE BOX!

Fun with Color

Cheerful pops of aqua and teal complement traditional holiday elements like a trimmed tree and sprigs of greenery. These playful vintage treasures—an aqua fan, fanciful figurines, and even a curious microscope—take a cozy living room's merriment up a whimsical notch.

The star of the festive affair is this creative tree topper folded into a measurably magnificent star. Bend a hinged ruler to shape, then apply a few drops of glue to secure the star into a permanent design sure to set a playful tone.

Links of Love

Pretty papers linked with love make a crafty chain to drape in halls, on stair rails, or even on thin branches. Creamy white can be quite striking, while newsprint, scrapbook sheets, or even playing cards can be fun choices too.

Meet me under the mistletoe! A cozy bench with room for two offers a sweet spot to catch a smooch.

Tiny Touches

A little whimsy goes a long way in decorating. *Clockwise from top left,* Vintage canning jars become homemade snow globes when filled with fluffy white flakes. A paper chain ringing the tree commands attention. Beloved ornaments have a place of honor on the tree or in a bowl while a set of lime dishes sparks a merry mood when stacked ready for a cup of cocoa.

Light and Airy

THIS QUIET COTTAGE IS BLANKETED IN SNOW,
EVEN IF A WHITE CHRISTMAS PASSES IT BY.
PEACEFUL, SOFT, AND SWEET, THIS HOME IS
FILLED WITH THE GENTLEST CHRISTMAS SPIRIT.

Winter Wonderland

A close look at the collectibles throughout this whitewashed cottage shows figurines, linens, and keepsakes in varying shades of white and ivory. Silver goblets and gold ornaments add contrasting color that illuminates the white even more. The emphasis is on a snowy Christmas with white trees, snowballs, snowmen, and snow globes throughout. Even white stockings are hung from a white chimney and filled with white snowmen and goodies.

Magical Place

A MAGICAL
CHRISTMAS AWAITS
INSIDE THIS CHEERY
LOG HOME. FROM THE
FRONT ENTRANCE,
BRIGHTLY COLORED
LIGHTS EXTEND A
GREETING TO A MERRY
HOLIDAY GATHERING
IN THE WOODS.

Cozy Dining

The intimate family dining room aglow with lamplight, a gathering of Christmas candles, and a rustic chandelier are cozy and comfortable. Seasonal china and sparkling crystal stand ready for a special Christmas Eve feast around the large farm table. Plenty of chairs assure that every member of this large family can share the joy of being home, together, for the holidays.

This cottage is surrounded by the serenity only nature can offer. Inside, the rooms are warm and inviting, dressed in their holiday best for special family celebrations. Fresh greenery gathered nearby frames the front door and inside adorns the mantel and the banister. It enhances candle wreaths large and small and adds a holiday touch to vintage pieces in almost every room. The big, beautiful tree, the star of the show, embodies the holiday spirit.

Take a look outside your home to find fresh greenery for the fireplace. Here it enhances a nativity scene on the mantel and drapes beautifully under layers of candles and over the fire's glow.

Childlike Joy

CHRISTMAS THROUGH THE EYES OF A
CHILD IS A JOYOUS TIME OF MAGIC AND
WONDER, THE STUFF VIVID MEMORIES
ARE MADE OF. UNWRAPPING A SPECIAL
ORNAMENT OR FINDING A FAVORITE
RECIPE EVOKES CHERISHED MEMORIES,
AND HEARTS ARE GLAD AT THE COMING
OF THIS SPECIAL SEASON.

Beloved symbols of the Christmas season are the focus of this charming home. Nativity scenes, jolly Santas, stockings at the mantel, and a carved box filled with shiny baubles fascinate little ones and recall holiday celebrations of long ago. A special tree on the screened porch, filled with birds and winter foliage, stands next to a diminutive rocking chair, where a child might keep watch on Christmas Eve through sleepy eyes.

A Fairy-tale Setting

THIS QUAINT ENGLISH-TUDOR
COTTAGE TUCKED UNDER STRETCHED
VINES IS ALMOST HIDDEN BEHIND A
MOSSY WALL. BUT INSIDE, BEAUTIFUL
HOLIDAY TREASURES COME ALIVE.

This warm home exudes classic charm. Nothing is overdone, yet every nook and cranny tell of the Christmas season. Fresh greenery and natural fruits and berries are used throughout, with each space boasting its own special touch of luxurious ribbon, colorful tassels, decorative candles, or quaint Christmas stockings.

Trimming Trees

JUST AS EACH HOME AND FAMILY HAS A UNIQUE, BEAUTIFUL PERSONALITY, SO DO THE TREES FILLING LIVING ROOMS AT CHRISTMASTIME.

Exquisite ornaments, beaded garland, and gauzy ribbon in browns and golds reflect the existing color palette of the room. Pops of bright color add seasonal sparkle.

Oversize red ribbon plays hide-and-seek in the branches of a stately tree, accenting the time-honored traditional color scheme of the season. Here, the ornaments are like pages of a scrapbook, each with a beloved story to tell: first Christmases, handmade art, favorite teachers, and more.

Charming Elegance

When decorating the tree, work off the existing colors and style of the room. Here, the same reds and oranges in the furniture show up on the tree, and even packages are wrapped to perfectly match the color scheme.

Bowl of Cheer

LIKE A DANCER TAKING HER PLACE MID STAGE, CENTERPIECES GRAB THE SPOTLIGHT ON A HOLIDAY TABLE. HERE ARE TWO SIMPLE YET STUNNING IDEAS.

Coming up Roses

What a lovely excuse to shine the silver! Fill a footed bowl with a bouquet of colorful mistletoe, berries, holly, and even fragrant rosemary. Then, up the elegance ante with showy ruby roses.

Snowy White

Set the scene for a winter wonderland. A crisp white palette accented with natural fibers, snowy pinecones, and even a flicker of light creates a seasonal setting that's calm, bright, and inviting.

Gifts & Ideas to Make
MEMORIES

Christmas is a time for giving, and it's also a time for baking and creating. Every family has its traditional holiday recipes, but finding new ones to create cherished memories is always enjoyable. Unique handcrafted gifts remind those lucky enough to receive them how much you care.

Goodies to Give

IT'S HARD TO FIND A MORE DELICIOUS WAY
TO DELIGHT IN THE SEASON OF GIVING THAN
OPENING YOUR HEART—AND YOUR KITCHEN—
TO THE ART OF THE HOMEMADE.

ORANGE CURD
Small canning jars can be embellished
with a cutout circle of metallic paper
placed under the lid. Complete the look
with a perky ribbon tied around the rim.

CINNAMON BEAR SNACK MIX
Clear or metallic pails with
handles hold several cups of
a merry snack mix.

Pepper-Jack Breadsticks

Makes 16 breadsticks

⅔ cup all-purpose flour
¼ cup yellow cornmeal
½ teaspoon sugar
¼ teaspoon baking soda
¼ teaspoon garlic salt
3 tablespoons chilled butter, cut into
    small pieces
½ cup shredded Monterey Jack
    cheese with peppers
¼ cup cold water
1 tablespoon white vinegar

1. In the work bowl of a food processor, place flour, cornmeal, sugar, baking soda, and garlic salt. Pulse 3 times or until combined. Add butter; pulse 3 times or until mixture is crumbly. Add cheese, water, and vinegar; pulse just until mixture forms a soft dough. On a lightly floured surface, knead 2 times. Divide in half. Wrap each portion of dough with plastic wrap; chill 1 hour or until firm.

2. Preheat oven to 375°. Line a baking sheet with parchment paper. Working with one portion of dough at a time (keep remaining dough refrigerated until ready to use), divide dough into 8 balls. On a lightly floured surface, roll each ball into an 8-inch rope. Place ropes, 1 inch apart, onto prepared baking sheet.

3. Bake for 10 minutes or until golden brown. Cool completely on

a wire rack. Repeat procedure with remaining dough.

Gumdrop Cookie Bites

Makes about 5 dozen cookies

1 (17.5-ounce) bag sugar cookie mix
½ cup butter, softened
1 large egg
1 teaspoon peppermint extract
1 cup small assorted-color
    gumdrops, coarsely chopped
    (see tip)
Confectioners' sugar

1. Preheat oven to 375°. Line mini muffin pans with paper liners. In a large bowl, combine cookie mix, butter, egg, peppermint extract, and chopped gumdrops; stir until well blended. Roll dough into about 1-inch balls; place one ball in each muffin cup (do not overfill cups).

2. Bake for 8 to 10 minutes or until lightly browned. Cool in pans for 5

minutes. Remove from pans, and cool completely on a wire rack. Just before serving, sprinkle with confectioners' sugar.

Tip: Use kitchen scissors to snip gumdrops into pieces.

Orange Curd

Makes about 2¼ cups

⅔ cup fresh orange juice
½ cup sugar
⅛ teaspoon salt
12 egg yolks
½ cup chilled butter, cut into
    8 pieces
2 teaspoons orange zest
½ teaspoon vanilla extract

1. In a medium, heavy-bottom saucepan, combine orange juice, sugar, and salt; stir just until sugar is moistened. Bring to a simmer over medium heat; remove from heat.

2. Gradually whisk ½ cup hot sugar mixture into egg yolks. Whisk egg yolk mixture into remaining hot sugar mixture in saucepan, whisking constantly. Cook over medium heat until thickened, whisking constantly, about 2 minutes. Remove from heat.

3. Gradually add butter, one piece at a time, stirring until melted. Stir in orange zest and vanilla. Pour into a bowl. Place a sheet of plastic wrap directly onto warm curd to prevent a film from forming. Chill until thickened, about 6 hours.

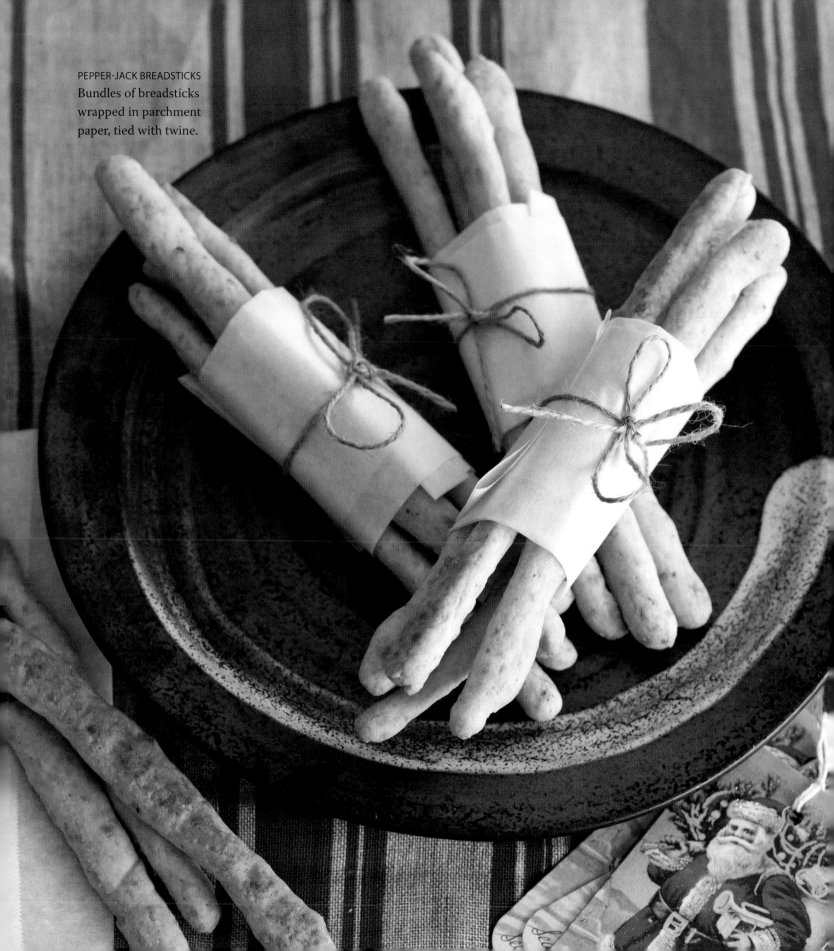

PEPPER-JACK BREADSTICKS
Bundles of breadsticks wrapped in parchment paper, tied with twine.

Cinnamon Bear Snack Mix
Makes about 22 cups

10 cups crispy corn-and-rice cereal
   squares
6 cups pretzel sticks
2 cups salted peanuts
2 cups chewy cinnamon bear candies
1½ cups green candy-coated
   chocolate pieces*
1½ cups white candy-coated
   chocolate pieces*
12 ounces white chocolate, finely
   chopped

1. In a large container, combine
cereal, pretzel sticks, peanuts, bear
candies, and green and white candy-
coated pieces.

2. In a medium microwave-safe
bowl, microwave white chocolate
on HIGH, in 30-second intervals,
stirring between each, until chocolate
is melted and smooth (about 1½
minutes total). Pour over cereal
mixture, stirring gently to coat evenly.

*We used M&M's.

Sun-dried Tomato Vinaigrette
Makes about 2½ cups

1½ cups apple cider
¾ cup water
½ cup sun-dried tomato paste with
 oil and spices
¼ teaspoon smoked paprika
1 teaspoon minced fresh rosemary

1. In the container of a blender, combine apple cider, water, sun-dried tomato paste, and smoked paprika; process until well blended. Stir in rosemary. Pour into a jar, and chill up to 1 week.

Buttery Garlic Croutons
Makes about 5 cups

5 cups (1-inch) cubed French bread
¼ cup butter, melted
½ teaspoon garlic powder
¼ teaspoon ground red pepper or
 to taste

1. Preheat oven to 350°. On a large rimmed baking sheet, place bread. Drizzle with butter. Sprinkle with garlic powder and red pepper; toss well. Bake for 12 minutes or until crisp and golden brown, stirring occasionally. Cool completely.

Home Made

The joy that you give to others is the joy that comes back to you.

Chocolate Hazelnut Cookie Truffles
Makes about 3 dozen truffles

1 (9-ounce) box chocolate wafers
1 cup hazelnuts
1 cup chocolate hazelnut spread*
½ cup butter, softened
21 ounces milk chocolate, finely
  chopped
Garnish: chopped hazelnuts

1. In the work bowl of a food processor, pulse cookies until finely chopped. In a large bowl, place crushed cookies.

2. In the work bowl of a food processor, pulse hazelnuts until finely chopped. Add hazelnuts to crushed cookies. Add chocolate hazelnut spread and softened butter to cookie mixture, mixing well. Chill for 1 hour. Roll into 1-inch balls. Freeze for 1 hour.

3. In a medium microwave-safe bowl, microwave chocolate on HIGH, in 30-second intervals, stirring between each, until chocolate is melted and smooth (about 1½ minutes total).

4. Line a rimmed baking sheet with parchment paper. Dip cookie balls into melted chocolate, allowing excess to drip off. Place on prepared baking sheet to cool. Garnish with chopped hazelnuts, if desired.

*We used Nutella.

Almond Cookie Truffles
Makes about 3 dozen truffles

1 (7-ounce) bag amaretti cookies
1 cup toasted almond slivers
1 (8-ounce) package cream cheese,
  softened
21 ounces white chocolate, finely
  chopped
Garnish: almond slivers

1. In the work bowl of a food processor, pulse cookies until finely ground. In a large bowl, place crushed cookies.

2. In the work bowl of a food processor, pulse almonds until finely ground. Add almonds to crushed cookies, stirring well. Add cream cheese to cookie mixture, mixing well. Chill for 1 hour. Roll into 1-inch balls. Freeze for 1 hour.

3. In a medium microwave-safe bowl, microwave chocolate on HIGH, in 30-second intervals, stirring between each, until chocolate is melted and smooth (about 1½ minutes total).

4. Line a rimmed baking sheet with wax paper. Dip cookie balls into melted chocolate, allowing excess to drip off. Place on prepared baking sheet to cool. Garnish with almond slivers, if desired.

Homemade Granola Bars
Makes 18 bars

1 cup finely chopped pitted dates
1 cup firmly packed light brown
  sugar
1 cup chopped walnuts
½ cup unsalted butter, softened
1 large egg, beaten
2 cups crisp rice cereal
½ cup uncooked quick-cooking oats
1 tablespoon orange zest
1 teaspoon vanilla extract

1. Spray a 9x9-inch baking pan with nonstick cooking spray.

2. In a large saucepan, combine dates, brown sugar, walnuts, butter, and egg. Bring to a simmer over medium-high heat, stirring constantly. Reduce heat to medium, and simmer for 4 to 5 minutes, stirring constantly.

3. Remove pan from heat. Add rice cereal, oats, orange zest, and vanilla, stirring to combine. Cool for 5 to 10 minutes or until cool enough to handle.

4. Press evenly into prepared pan. Cool completely. Cut into 3x1½-inch bars.

Note: Bars may be made up to 4 days ahead. Store at room temperature in an airtight container.

Cranberry Cheddar Wafers

Makes about 8 dozen wafers

2 (8-ounce) blocks sharp Cheddar
cheese, shredded
1½ cups butter, softened
1 teaspoon salt
1 teaspoon ground red pepper
1 teaspoon smoked paprika
3 cups all-purpose flour
¾ cup finely ground pecans
½ cup sweetened dried cranberries

1. In the bowl of a heavy-duty stand mixer fitted with paddle attachment, combine cheese, butter, salt, red pepper, and paprika. Beat at medium speed until well blended. Gradually add flour, beating until combined. Add pecans and cranberries, beating to combine. Cover tightly, and chill for 2 hours.

2. Shape dough into 5-inch logs. Wrap each tightly with plastic wrap, and chill for 4 hours.

3. Preheat oven to 350°. Line several baking sheets with parchment paper. Slice logs into ¼-inch slices. Bake for 10 to 12 minutes or until lightly golden. Cool on pans for 2 to 3 minutes. Remove from pans, and cool completely on wire racks.

Raspberry Swirl Cheesecake Bars

Makes 9 bars

Crust:
1¼ cups all-purpose flour
½ cup firmly packed brown sugar
¼ cup uncooked quick-cooking oats
¼ cup chopped pecans or walnuts
¼ teaspoon ground cinnamon
⅛ teaspoon salt
½ cup chilled butter, cut into small
   pieces

Filling:
2 (8-ounce) packages cream cheese,
   softened
½ cup sugar
2 tablespoons all-purpose flour
1 large egg
½ teaspoon lemon zest
½ teaspoon vanilla extract
⅓ cup seedless raspberry preserves

1. Preheat oven to 350°. Line an 8-inch square baking pan with aluminum foil, allowing foil to extend 2 inches over edges of pan; lightly spray foil with nonstick baking spray with flour.

2. To prepare crust: In the work bowl of a food processor, combine 1¼ cups flour, sugar, oats, nuts, cinnamon, and salt; pulse 2 times. Add butter; pulse 4 or 5 times or until crumbly. Press mixture into bottom of prepared pan. Bake for 12 minutes (center will not be completely set). Cool for 10 minutes on a wire rack.

3. To prepare filling: In a large bowl, combine cream cheese, sugar, and 2 tablespoons flour; beat at medium speed with a mixer until smooth. Add egg, lemon zest, and vanilla; beat until blended. Spread over crust. Drop preserves by teaspoonsful over cream cheese mixture; lightly swirl with the tip of a knife.

4. Bake for 22 to 25 minutes or until cream cheese mixture is set. Cool in pan for 1 hour on a wire rack. Lightly cover with foil; chill thoroughly. Remove from pan using edges of foil as handles. Cut into bars.

Note: If preserves have been refrigerated, spoon into a bowl, and stir until smooth.

Pineapple-Coconut Mini Loaves
Makes 5 (6x3¼-inch) loaves

1 cup butter, softened
3 cups sugar
5 large eggs
¾ cup sour cream
1 (20-ounce) can pineapple chunks,
    drained and juice reserved
1 teaspoon vanilla extract
3 cups all-purpose flour
½ teaspoon baking powder
¼ teaspoon salt
¼ teaspoon baking soda
1 cup sweetened flaked coconut

1. Preheat oven to 300°. Spray 5 (6x3¼-inch) loaf pans with nonstick baking spray with flour.

2. In a large bowl, beat butter at medium-high speed with a mixer until creamy. Add sugar, beating for 2 to 3 minutes until fluffy. Add eggs, one at a time, beating well after each addition. Add sour cream, ¼ cup reserved pineapple juice, and vanilla, beating well.

3. In a large bowl, sift together flour, baking powder, salt, and baking soda. Add flour mixture to butter mixture, one cup at a time, beating well after each addition.

4. Chop 1 cup pineapple chunks into small pieces. Fold pineapple and coconut into batter.

5. Pour into prepared pans. Bake for 35 to 45 minutes or until a wooden pick inserted in center of each loaf comes out clean. Cool in pans for 10 minutes. Remove from pans, and cool completely on a wire rack.

Note: To make 1 (10-inch) cake, use a 12- to 15-cup Bundt pan. Bake at 300° for 1 hour to 1 hour and 15 minutes or until a wooden pick inserted in center of cake comes out clean.

2. In a medium bowl, whisk together sugar, butter, milk, salt, vanilla, and eggs. Place 2 tablespoons coconut in each prepared tart crust. Pour about ¼ cup egg mixture over coconut (do not overfill). Repeat procedure with remaining crusts and egg mixture. Place tart pans on a large rimmed baking sheet.

3. Bake for 15 minutes. Remove from oven; sprinkle with remaining coconut. Bake for 10 minutes longer or until crust is lightly browned and filling is set. Cool completely on a wire rack. Remove from tart pans.

Coconut Tarts
Makes about 8 tarts

1 (14.1-ounce) package refrigerated
　pie crusts
1½ cups sugar
¼ cup butter, melted
1 (5-ounce) can evaporated milk
⅛ teaspoon salt
1 teaspoon vanilla extract
2 large eggs
2 cups sweetened flaked coconut,
　divided

1. Preheat oven to 350°. On a lightly floured surface, unroll pie crusts. Cut 8 (4½-inch) rounds from pie crusts, rerolling scraps, if necessary. Fit rounds into 8 (4-inch) nonstick tart pans with removable bottoms, gently pressing dough on bottom and up sides of pans. Trim excess dough.

Gingerbread Men
Makes about 8 (5-inch) gingerbread

6 tablespoons butter, softened
¾ cup firmly packed dark brown
　sugar
½ cup unsulfured molasses
1 large egg
3 cups all-purpose flour
2 teaspoons ground ginger
1½ teaspoons apple pie spice
¼ teaspoon baking powder

½ teaspoon salt
Prepared cookie icing
White and red dragées

1. In the bowl of a heavy-duty stand mixer fitted with paddle attachment, combine butter and sugar. Beat at medium speed until fluffy, stopping to scrape bowl occasionally. Add molasses and egg; beat until blended.

2. In a medium bowl, whisk together flour, ginger, apple pie spice, baking powder, and salt. Gradually add to butter mixture, beating until blended (dough will be thick). Place dough on a lightly floured surface; knead lightly 2 or 3 times to combine. Divide dough in half. Flatten each portion of dough into a 5-inch disk; wrap with plastic wrap. Chill 2 hours.

3. Preheat oven to 350°. Line a large baking sheet with parchment paper. On a lightly floured surface, unwrap one portion of dough. Using a lightly floured rolling pin, roll dough to about ¼-inch thickness. Cut dough with a 5-inch gingerbread man cutter. Reroll scraps as necessary. Using a spatula, place cutouts on prepared baking sheet.

4. Bake for 12 minutes or until edges begin to feel firm and cookies are lightly browned. Remove from oven; cool on pan for 2 minutes. Remove from pan, and cool completely on a wire rack. Repeat procedure with remaining portion of dough. Decorate as desired using cookie icing and dragées.

Cranberry-Raspberry Liqueur

Makes 1 quart

2 cups sugar

1 cup water

1 (12-ounce) package fresh cranberries, chopped

1 cup fresh raspberries

1 (3-inch) vanilla bean, split lengthwise

3 cups vodka

Garnish: fresh cranberries, and fresh raspberries

1. In a medium saucepan, combine sugar and water; bring to a simmer over medium-low heat. Cook 3 minutes or until sugar dissolves, stirring occasionally. Remove from heat; cool completely.

2. In a large glass bowl, combine sugar mixture, cranberries, and raspberries. Scrape seeds from vanilla bean into cranberry mixture. Add vanilla bean. Stir in vodka. Cover and chill for 4 weeks, stirring occasionally.

3. Strain cranberry mixture through a fine-mesh sieve into a bowl; discard solids. Pour liqueur into clean bottles, leaving enough headspace to add additional fresh cranberries and fresh raspberries, if desired. Seal bottles, and store in refrigerator up to 5 months.

Note: Cranberries and raspberries used for garnish should be discarded after 1 month.

Paprika Popcorn

Makes about 20 servings

20 cups air-popped popcorn
2 cups golden raisins
2 cups raisins
1½ cups sunflower seeds
½ cup extra-virgin olive oil
4 teaspoons seasoned salt
1 teaspoon ground cumin
1 teaspoon ground chipotle chile
  pepper
1 teaspoon smoked paprika
1 teaspoon turmeric

1. Preheat oven to 200°.

2. In a large roasting pan, place popcorn, raisins, and sunflower seeds. Drizzle with olive oil, stirring until popcorn is evenly coated.

3. In a medium bowl, combine seasoned salt, cumin, chipotle pepper, paprika, and turmeric. Sprinkle over popcorn mixture, stirring evenly to coat.

4. Bake for 1 hour, stirring every 15 minutes. Immediately spread popcorn onto parchment paper to cool. Store in an airtight container.

Herbed Cheese Log

Makes 2 (6-inch) logs

2 (8-ounce) packages cream cheese,
  softened
½ cup butter, softened
½ cup dried parsley
¼ cup Italian seasoning
¼ cup dried chives
1 tablespoon crushed red pepper
½ teaspoon garlic powder

1. In a large bowl, combine cream cheese and butter. Beat at medium speed with a mixer until smooth.

2. In a medium bowl, combine parsley, Italian seasoning, chives, crushed red pepper, and garlic powder. Add ¼ cup dried herb mixture to cream cheese mixture, beating until smooth. Cover tightly, and chill for 1 hour or until firm.

3. Shape cream cheese mixture into 2 (6-inch) logs. Roll in remaining herb mixture. Wrap tightly with plastic wrap or parchment paper, securing ends, and chill until firm.

Note: Store logs in refrigerator up to 5 days.

Heavenly Treats

PILED-HIGH STACKS OF SWEETS ARE A
DIVINE SIGHT AT ANY PARTY. WRAP THEM
IN A LOVELY TO-GO PACKAGE FOR FRIENDS
TO TAKE HOME, OR BRING A VARIETY TO THE
OFFICE OR SCHOOL FOR A DELICIOUS WAY
TO TREAT COWORKERS AND TEACHERS.

Lemon Squares

Makes about 40 (1½-inch) squares

2¼ cups plus 6 tablespoons all-
   purpose flour, divided
¾ cup almond flour*
¾ cup plus 3 tablespoons
   confectioners' sugar, divided
¼ teaspoon salt
¾ cup unsalted butter, softened
4 large eggs
1¾ cups sugar
1½ tablespoons lemon zest
2 tablespoons fresh lemon juice
1 teaspoon baking powder
½ teaspoon vanilla extract

1. Preheat oven to 350°. Line a 13x9-inch baking pan with aluminum foil, allowing foil to extend 2 inches over edges of pan. Spray foil with nonstick cooking spray.

2. In a medium bowl, sift together 2¼ cups all-purpose flour, almond flour, ¾ cup confectioners' sugar, and salt. Using a pastry blender, cut in butter until mixture is crumbly. Press firmly into prepared pan. Bake for 15 to 20 minutes or until mixture is lightly browned.

3. In a large bowl, beat eggs at medium speed with a mixer for 1 minute. Add remaining 6 tablespoons all-purpose flour, sugar, lemon zest and juice, baking powder, and vanilla, beating until smooth. Pour filling over hot crust.

4. Bake for 15 to 20 minutes or until set. Cool completely in pan. Remove from pan using edges of foil as handles. Dust top with remaining 3 tablespoons confectioners' sugar. Cut into squares.

*We used Bob's Red Mill Almond Flour.

Red Velvet Cupcakes

Makes 36 mini cupcakes

3 tablespoons unsalted butter,
   softened
3 tablespoons vegetable shortening
⅔ cup sugar
2 large eggs
1⅓ cups all-purpose flour
2 tablespoons unsweetened cocoa
   powder
½ teaspoon baking soda
½ teaspoon salt
½ cup buttermilk
2 tablespoons red liquid food
   coloring
1 teaspoon white vinegar
½ teaspoon vanilla extract
Cream Cheese Frosting
   (recipe follows)
Red velvet cake crumbles, optional

1. Preheat oven to 325°. Line 3 (12-cup) mini muffin pans with paper liners.

2. In a large bowl, beat butter and shortening at medium speed with a mixer until creamy. Add sugar, and beat until fluffy. Add eggs, one at a time, beating well after each addition.

3. In another medium bowl, sift together flour, cocoa powder, baking soda, and salt. In a small bowl, combine buttermilk and food coloring. Gradually add flour mixture to sugar mixture alternately with buttermilk mixture, beginning and ending with flour mixture, beating just until combined after each addition. Add vinegar and vanilla, beating until blended.

4. Spoon batter into prepared pans, filling each two-thirds full. Bake for 15 to 20 minutes or until a wooden pick inserted in center comes out clean. Cool in pans for 10 minutes. Remove from pans, and cool completely on wire racks.

5. Spread Cream Cheese Frosting over cooled cupcakes. Garnish with cake crumbles, if desired.

Cream Cheese Frosting

Makes about 2¼ cups

1 (8-ounce) package cream cheese,
   softened
2 teaspoons buttermilk
3 cups confectioners' sugar

1. In a large bowl, beat cream cheese and buttermilk at medium speed with a mixer until creamy. Gradually add confectioners' sugar, beating until smooth.

Wrapped to Go

GIFTS FASHIONED WITH TIME, ENERGY, AND LOVE ARE THE ONES THAT ARE CHERISHED LONG AFTER THE HUSTLE AND BUSTLE IS OVER. CREATIVE GIFTS SHOW THOSE MOST SPECIAL JUST HOW MUCH YOU APPRECIATE THEM.

MERINGUE SURPRISES

Gifts & Ideas to Make Memories   183

3. Roll dough into 1-inch balls, and place on prepared baking sheets. Bake for 17 to 20 minutes or just until edges are golden brown. Sift confectioners' sugar over hot cookies. Cool on pans for 3 minutes. Remove from pans, and cool completely on wire racks.

4. Sift a second coating of confectioners' sugar over cooled cookies. Store in airtight containers up to 1 week, or freeze up to 1 month.

Hello Dolly Bars
Makes about 2 dozen bars

½ cup butter, melted
1 cup graham cracker crumbs
1 cup sweetened flaked coconut
1 cup semisweet chocolate morsels
1 cup chopped pecans
1 (14-ounce) can sweetened
  condensed milk

1. Preheat oven to 350°. Line an 8-inch square pan with aluminum foil, allowing foil to extend several inches over edges of pan.

2. In a large bowl, combine butter and graham cracker crumbs. Press firmly into prepared pan. Add coconut, chocolate morsels, and pecans, in layers, to completely cover crust.

3. Drizzle sweetened condensed milk over top.

4. Bake for 30 minutes. Cool in pan on a wire rack. Remove from pan, using foil as handles. Cut into bars.

Meringue Surprises
Makes about 30 cookies

4 egg whites, room temperature
½ teaspoon salt
½ teaspoon cream of tartar
2 teaspoons vanilla extract
1½ cups sugar
1½ cups chopped nuts
1 (12-ounce) package semisweet
  chocolate morsels

1. Preheat oven to 300°. Line baking sheets with parchment paper.

2. In a large bowl, beat egg whites at medium speed with a mixer until foamy. Add salt, cream of tartar, and vanilla, beating until soft peaks form. Gradually add sugar, 1 tablespoon at a time, beating until stiff peaks form and sugar dissolves, 2 to 4 minutes. Fold in nuts and chocolate morsels.

3. Pipe or dollop mixture, about 2 tablespoons for each, onto prepared pans about 1 inch apart. Bake for 25 minutes. Cool completely, and store in airtight containers.

Karen's Cocoons
Makes 5 dozen cookies

1 cup butter, softened
2¼ cups all-purpose flour
¼ cup confectioners' sugar
2 cups chopped pecans
2 teaspoons vanilla extract
Confectioners' sugar

1. Preheat oven to 350°. Line baking sheets with parchment paper.

2. In a large bowl, beat butter at medium speed with a mixer until creamy. In a medium bowl, combine flour and sugar. Add flour mixture to butter mixture, beating until creamy. Add pecans and vanilla, beating until blended.

Oatmeal Cookies
Makes about 3 dozen cookies

1 cup vegetable shortening
¾ cup sugar
¾ cup firmly packed light brown
   sugar
1 large egg
¼ cup water
1 teaspoon vanilla extract
½ teaspoon ground cinnamon
1 cup self-rising flour
3¼ cups quick-cooking oats

1. Preheat oven to 350°. Spray baking sheets with nonstick baking spray with flour.

2. In a large bowl, beat shortening, sugar, and light brown sugar with a mixer until fluffy. Add egg, water, vanilla, and cinnamon, beating until blended. Add flour, beating until combined. Stir in oats.

3. Drop by teaspoonfuls onto prepared pans. Bake for 10 minutes or until edges begin to brown. Cool on pans for 3 minutes. Remove from pans, and cool completely on wire racks.

Spice of Life

SOME SPICES ECHO THE SCENT OF CHRISTMAS AND THE COMFORT AND WARMTH OF HOME. MIX SWEET-SMELLING SPICES FOR HOMEMADE HOLIDAY GIFTS TO CAPTURE THE ESSENCE OF THE SEASON.

SPICED CHOCOLATE TRUFFLES

Enjoy a mug of this steaming tea by a roaring fireplace.

Spiced Jam Tartlets

Makes 24 mini tarts

1 cup all-purpose flour
1 tablespoon sugar
½ teaspoon ground cinnamon
¼ teaspoon ground ginger
¼ teaspoon ground allspice
⅛ teaspoon salt
¼ cup (2 ounces) cream cheese, softened
2 tablespoons unsalted butter, softened
2 tablespoons milk
¾ cup fruit jam, such as fig, pear, or apple
Garnish: dried fruit and raisins

1. In a medium bowl, whisk together flour, sugar, cinnamon, ginger, allspice, and salt. In another medium bowl, beat cream cheese and butter at medium-high speed with a mixer until smooth and creamy.

2. Reduce mixer speed to low, and slowly add flour mixture and milk to cream cheese mixture; beat until mixture is crumbly. On a lightly floured surface, form into a disk, and wrap tightly with plastic wrap. Chill for 2 hours.

3. Preheat oven to 350°. Spray 2 (12-cup) mini muffin pans with nonstick cooking spray; set aside.

4. Unwrap dough, and place on a lightly floured surface; knead 3 or 4 times.

Divide dough into 24 equal portions, and place 1 piece of dough into each muffin cup, pressing into bottom and up sides.

5. Spoon 1½ teaspoons jam into each dough cup. Bake for 20 minutes or until crusts are light brown. Cool in pans for 10 minutes; remove from pans, and cool completely on wire racks. Garnish with dried fruit and raisins, if desired.

Spiced Chocolate Truffles

Makes about 48 truffles

12 (1-ounce) squares bittersweet chocolate, chopped
9 (1-ounce) squares semisweet chocolate, chopped
½ teaspoon ground cinnamon
¼ teaspoon ground chipotle chile pepper
½ teaspoon dried orange zest
¼ teaspoon ground cardamom
½ teaspoon finely minced fresh ginger
¼ teaspoon ground ginger
½ cup heavy cream
½ cup whole milk
¼ cup confectioners' sugar
2 (16-ounce) packages chocolate-flavored candy coating, melted
Garnish: ground chipotle chile pepper, candied orange zest, and candied ginger

1. In a medium bowl, combine chopped chocolates. Evenly divide chocolate mixture among 3 small bowls.

2. In first bowl, add cinnamon and chipotle pepper. In second bowl, add orange zest and cardamom. In third bowl, add fresh ginger and ground ginger.

3. In a medium saucepan, combine cream, milk, and confectioners' sugar. Bring to a boil; remove from heat. Evenly divide the hot cream mixture among the 3 bowls of chocolate and spices, whisking gently until chocolate is completely melted. Cover each bowl tightly with plastic wrap; set aside to cool, and then freeze until thoroughly chilled.

4. Line 3 rimmed baking sheets with parchment paper; set aside.

5. Using a 1-inch spring-loaded scoop, scoop chocolate mixture into hands, and roll into a ball. (Work quickly to prevent chocolate from softening.) Transfer to prepared baking sheets, keeping each flavor separate. Using 2 forks, dip truffles into melted candy coating, allowing excess to drip off, and place on prepared baking sheets. Garnish truffles according to flavor, if desired. Store in an airtight container for up to one week.

Holiday Tea

Makes about 1 cup loose-leaf tea
for 24 individual servings

2 tablespoons dried orange zest
1 tablespoon ground ginger
24 whole cloves
2 to 4 whole star anise pods
½ cup loose-leaf black tea*

1. In a large bowl, combine orange
zest, ginger, cloves, star anise, and
tea leaves; stir well to combine. Place
in a decorative bag for gift-giving,
if desired. If dividing the mixture for
several gifts, include a star anise pod
in each bag.

*We used Bigelow English Breakfast
loose tea.

Fresh Tidings

IT'S THE SEASON TO MAKE MERRY, AND THERE'S NO DOUBT
YOUR HOLIDAY DATEBOOK IS PACKED WITH PARTIES!
DON'T BE CAUGHT EMPTY-HANDED. HERE WE OFFER
SIMPLE GIFT IDEAS PERFECT FOR EVERY HAPPY HOSTESS.

Gourmet Gift

Fresh herbs are the gift that keeps on giving. Easy-to-care-for herbs add flavor and complement almost any dish. Package a pretty plant in paper (and even add a hand-scripted recipe) for the perfect present.

WISPY THYME IN A DECOMPOSABLE POT IS VEILED IN NEWSPRINT AND SECURED WITH TWINE.

Wrapped Up

Make a homemade gift even more special by spending a few extra minutes perfecting the packaging. Bonus points for adding bling—especially in the form of an ornate ornament!

THIS GLASS CONTAINER FILLED WITH WHOLE MIXED NUTS IS WRAPPED IN SPARKLY SILVER MESH FABRIC AND TIED WITH A BRIGHT BOW ACCENTED BY A KEEPSAKE ORNAMENT.

White Out

There's something about white
that's clean and classic. Turn a few
simple pots into showy planters by
whitewashing the terra-cotta with
paint for the perfect foil for herbs.

Treats & Cheers

Clever goblets made from jars and
candlesticks do double duty when filled
with favorite nibbles. Granola, dried
fruits, and nuts make colorful—and
quick—treats. After the goodies are
gone, the glasses are perfect for sipping!

Ready to Roll

A weathered milk crate makes a striking carrier. Please all the senses by selecting a variety of fresh herbs—rosemary, mint, oregano, and sage are popular picks. Then add a decorative label—chalkboard is classic—for easy identification. These fragrant plants also make fabulous favors for dinner parties. Dig in!

Toast the Host
The tried-and-true gift of wine is still a sure bet. Sweeten the sentiment by adding a decorative stopper, which can be found in festive shapes and sizes.

Treasure Box of
RECIPES

'Tis the season to be jolly, whether at a merry
luncheon or a cocktail party. Easy to transport—
and even easier to share—our trove of tasty treats,
scrumptious cakes, and indulgent beverages
provides riches for a season's worth of celebrations.

Spice Cake with Fluffy White Frosting

Makes 1 (8-inch) cake

1 (18.25-ounce) box classic white
   cake mix
1 cup water
⅓ cup canola oil
1½ teaspoons ground cinnamon
½ teaspoon ground nutmeg
1 tablespoon orange zest, divided
Fluffy White Frosting (recipe follows)
1 cup pecan halves, chopped and
   toasted
Garnish: chopped toasted pecans
   and Sugared Fruit and Rosemary
   (recipe follows)

1. Preheat oven to 350°. Lightly coat the bottoms of 3 (8-inch) round cake pans with nonstick baking spray with flour.

2. In a large bowl, combine cake mix, water, oil, cinnamon, nutmeg, and 1 teaspoon orange zest. Stir just until moistened. Beat at medium speed with a mixer for 2 minutes. Divide batter evenly among prepared pans.

3. Bake for 18 to 20 minutes or until a wooden pick inserted in center comes out clean. Cool in pans on wire racks for 10 minutes. Run a knife around edges of pans. Invert cakes onto wire racks. Cool completely.

4. In a medium bowl, place 2½ cups Fluffy White Frosting; gently fold in 1 cup chopped pecans and remaining 2 teaspoons orange zest. On a cake plate, place 1 cake layer; top with half of pecan frosting mixture, spreading to edges of cake layer. Top with another cake layer, spreading with remaining pecan frosting mixture. Top with remaining cake layer. Spread remaining Fluffy White Frosting over top and sides of cake. Garnish with additional pecans and Sugared Fruit and Rosemary, if desired.

Fluffy White Frosting

Makes about 6 cups

1 cup plus 3 tablespoons sugar,
   divided
⅓ cup water
1 tablespoon light corn syrup
⅛ teaspoon salt
¼ teaspoon cream of tartar
4 egg whites
1 teaspoon vanilla extract

1. In a small, heavy-bottom saucepan, combine 1 cup sugar, water, corn syrup, and salt; swirl saucepan to moisten sugar. Bring to a boil over medium-high heat, stirring just until sugar dissolves. Cook, without stirring, until a candy thermometer registers 240° (about 5 minutes). Remove from heat.

2. In the bowl of a heavy-duty stand mixer fitted with whisk attachment, combine cream of tartar and egg whites. Beat at high speed until egg whites are foamy. Gradually add remaining 3 tablespoons sugar, beating just until medium peaks form.

3. With mixer on medium speed, slowly pour hot syrup into egg whites. Increase speed to high; beat just until stiff peaks form. Beat in vanilla. Use immediately.

Sugared Fruit and Rosemary

1 or 2 tangerines, sliced crosswise
   into rounds
Fresh whole cranberries
1 small Lady apple or whole
   tangerine
Fresh rosemary sprigs
¼ cup water
1 envelope unflavored gelatin
Sugar

1. Allow tangerines slices to dry at room temperature for several hours. Gently pat cut surfaces dry with a paper towel.

2. Rinse remaining fruit and rosemary, and gently pat dry. Place a wire rack over a sheet of wax paper.

3. In a small saucepan, place water; sprinkle with gelatin. Let stand for 2 minutes or until softened. Cook over low heat, stirring frequently, until gelatin dissolves. Pour gelatin into a small bowl; whisk until slightly foamy.

4. Using a small, clean paintbrush, spread a thin coat of gelatin over fruit and rosemary. Sprinkle with sugar. Place on prepared wire rack, and let stand in a cool, dry place until set, about 3 hours; do not refrigerate. Sprinkle any damp spots with more sugar until desired effect is achieved.

Tip: Begin beating cream of tartar and egg whites when candy thermometer reaches about 235°. The goal is to have the medium-peak egg whites ready just when the sugar syrup reaches 240°.

Dazzling Display When setting up your cake station, keep in mind the cakes themselves will serve as the primary decoration. Seasonal greenery, lengths of ribbon, a few fresh flowers, and perhaps a festive runner for the sideboard or display table are all that's required for an elegant yet dazzling presentation.

A tempting torte tower takes dessert to all new heights.

Bittersweet Mocha Torte

Makes 1 torte

3 (1-ounce) squares unsweetened baking chocolate
1 cup butter
1 cup sour cream
¼ teaspoon baking soda
3 cups sugar
6 large eggs, separated
1 teaspoon vanilla extract
3 cups all-purpose flour
1 teaspoon salt
2 tablespoons powdered mocha coffee drink mix
Chocolate Mousse (recipe follows)
Bittersweet Chocolate Sauce (recipe follows)
Confectioners' sugar

1. In a medium microwave-safe bowl, microwave chocolate and butter on High until melted, about 2 minutes. Stir until smooth. Cool.

2. Preheat oven to 325°. Spray 2 (9x5-inch) loaf pans with nonstick baking spray with flour.

3. In a small bowl, combine sour cream and baking soda.

4. In a large bowl, beat chocolate mixture and sugar at medium speed with a mixer until fluffy. Add egg yolks, one at a time, beating well after each addition. Add vanilla, beating to mix well.

5. Reduce mixer speed to low. In a separate bowl, sift together flour, salt, and mocha coffee drink mix 3 times. Add flour mixture to chocolate mixture alternately with sour cream mixture, beginning and ending with flour mixture, blending well after each addition.

6. In a separate bowl, beat egg whites at high speed with a mixer until stiff peaks form. Fold egg whites into batter until well combined.

7. Spoon batter into prepared pans. Bake for 30 minutes; remove pans from oven. Cover loosely with aluminum foil to prevent excessive browning. Bake for 35 to 40 minutes longer or until a wooden pick inserted in center comes out clean. Cool in pans for 10 minutes. Remove from pans; cool completely on a wire rack.

8. Trim off domed portion of each cake. Cut cakes in half horizontally to create 2 layers each. Spread Chocolate Mousse between cake layers.

9. Wrap torte with heavy-duty plastic wrap; freeze for 2 hours. Using an electric knife, trim ½ inch off ends and sides of cake to make an 8x4-inch rectangle.

10. Drizzle with warm Bittersweet Chocolate Sauce. Garnish with confectioners' sugar, if desired.

Chocolate Mousse

Makes about 3 cups

1½ cups heavy cream
2 tablespoons light corn syrup
16 (1-ounce) squares semisweet baking chocolate, coarsely chopped
2 tablespoons butter

1. In a medium saucepan, combine heavy cream and corn syrup. Bring to boil over medium heat; remove from heat. Add chocolate and butter, stirring until smooth.

2. Cover and chill for 1 hour. Beat chocolate mixture at high speed with a mixer until soft peaks form.

Bittersweet Chocolate Sauce

Makes 2 cups

6 (1-ounce) squares bittersweet chocolate, chopped
½ cup butter
1 cup sugar
1 (5-ounce) can evaporated milk

1. In a medium saucepan over low heat, heat chocolate and butter, stirring until melted and smooth.

2. Stir in sugar and evaporated milk; simmer for 5 minutes, stirring constantly, until sugar is dissolved.

Hazelnut Meringue Torte

Makes 1 (8-inch) torte

6 egg whites, room temperature
½ teaspoon cream of tartar
½ cup sugar
½ cup finely chopped hazelnuts
1 envelope unflavored gelatin
3 tablespoons cold water
¼ cup boiling water
3 cups heavy cream
¼ cup sugar
¼ cup hazelnut liqueur
Garnish: fresh raspberries and
   confectioners' sugar

1. Preheat oven to 250°. Line 2 baking sheets with parchment paper. Draw 2 (8-inch) circles on one piece of parchment paper, and one 8-inch circle on the second sheet.

2. In a large bowl, beat egg whites and cream of tartar at high speed with a mixer until foamy. Gradually add sugar, 1 tablespoon at a time, beating until stiff peaks form and sugar dissolves, 2 to 4 minutes. Gently fold in hazelnuts.

3. Spoon or pipe meringue onto 8-inch circles on prepared baking sheets. Bake for 1 hour and 15 minutes. Turn off oven, and leave meringues in oven, with oven door closed, for 8 hours or until dry.

4. In a bowl, soften gelatin in cold water. Stir; let stand for 2 minutes. Add boiling water, stirring until gelatin dissolves.

5. In a large bowl, beat heavy cream at high speed with a mixer until thickened. Add sugar, 1 tablespoon at a time, beating until soft peaks form. Stir in gelatin mixture and hazelnut liqueur; cover and chill for 4 hours.

6. On a serving platter, place one meringue. Spoon or pipe one-third of cream mixture onto meringue. Top with second meringue and another third of cream mixture. Top with remaining meringue. Pipe top with remaining cream mixture.

7. Garnish with fresh raspberries and confectioners' sugar, if desired. Serve immediately.

Black Walnut Cake

Makes 1 (9-inch) cake

2 cups sugar
⅔ cup vegetable shortening
1 teaspoon vanilla extract
2¾ cups all-purpose flour
1 tablespoon baking powder
½ teaspoon salt
1 cup water
4 egg whites
½ teaspoon cream of tartar
1 cup chopped black walnuts
Black Walnut Icing (recipe follows)
Garnish: chopped black walnuts

1. Preheat oven to 350°. Spray 2 (9-inch) round cake pans with nonstick baking spray with flour.

2. In a large bowl, beat sugar and shortening at medium speed with a mixer until fluffy. Add vanilla, mixing well.

3. In a medium bowl, sift together flour, baking powder, and salt.

Gradually add flour mixture to shortening mixture alternately with water, beginning and ending with flour mixture, beating just until combined after each addition.

4. In a separate bowl, beat egg whites and cream of tartar at high speed with a mixer until stiff peaks form. Fold egg whites into batter until well combined. Stir in black walnuts. Pour batter evenly into prepared pans.

5. Bake for 27 to 30 minutes or until a wooden pick inserted in center comes out clean. Cool in pans for 10 minutes; remove from pans, and cool completely on wire racks.

6. Spread Black Walnut Icing between layers and on top and sides of cake. Garnish with chopped black walnuts, if desired.

Note: Store cake in refrigerator.

Black Walnut Icing

Makes 5½ cups

2½ cups heavy cream
⅓ cup sugar
¾ teaspoon vanilla extract
½ cup finely chopped black walnuts

1. In a medium bowl, combine heavy cream and sugar. Beat at medium speed with a mixer until soft peaks form.

2. Add vanilla, and beat until stiff peaks form. Fold in black walnuts.

3. Chill until ready to use.

Layer Cakes make wonderful Christmas gifts for friends, coworkers, and neighbors, but delivering them can present a challenge. Find a specialty supply store online or visit a local bakery to purchase a supply of cake boards and boxes. To keep the cake stable during transport, drizzle a bit of light corn syrup on the board before placing the cake on it. To add a festive touch, customize the boxes with holiday-themed stamps or adhesive designs and sturdy ribbon.

Christmas Cake
Makes 1 (8-inch) cake

1½ cups sugar
1¼ cups vegetable oil
3 large eggs
1 tablespoon orange liqueur
2¾ cups all-purpose flour
1 teaspoon baking soda
½ teaspoon salt
1 cup buttermilk
1 (18-ounce) jar sweet orange
   marmalade
Orange-Cranberry Filling (recipe follows)
Orange-Cream Cheese Frosting
  (recipe follows)
Garnish: orange zest strips

1. Preheat oven to 350°. Grease and flour 3 (8-inch) round cake pans.

2. In a large bowl, beat sugar, oil, eggs, and liqueur at medium speed with a mixer until smooth.

3. In a medium bowl, combine flour, baking soda, and salt. Gradually add flour mixture to sugar mixture alternately with buttermilk, beginning and ending with flour mixture, beating just until combined after each addition. Stir in marmalade.

4. Pour batter into prepared pans. Bake for 30 minutes or until a wooden pick inserted in center comes out clean. Cool in pans for 10 minutes. Remove from pans; cool completely on wire racks.

5. Spread ¾ cup Orange-Cranberry Filling over bottom and middle cake layers. Top with remaining cake layer.

Spread Orange-Cream Cheese Frosting on top and sides of cake, reserving a portion for piping a border, if desired. Spread remaining ¾ cup Orange-Cranberry Filling over top of cake. Pipe border around bottom and top of cake with reserved Orange-Cream Cheese Frosting, if desired. Garnish with orange zest strips, if desired.

Orange-Cranberry Filling
Makes 1½ cups

1 (14-ounce) can whole-berry
   cranberry sauce
2 tablespoons orange liqueur
1 tablespoon sugar

1. In a small saucepan, combine cranberry sauce, liqueur, and sugar. Simmer over medium heat, stirring constantly, for 10 minutes or until thickened; cool.

Orange-Cream Cheese Frosting
Makes about 4 cups

1 (8-ounce) package cream cheese,
   softened
½ cup butter, softened
2 tablespoons orange liqueur
1 tablespoon orange zest
6 cups confectioners' sugar

1. In a large bowl, combine cream cheese and butter. Beat at medium speed with a mixer until creamy.

2. Beat in liqueur and orange zest until combined. Gradually beat in confectioners' sugar until smooth.

Bûche de Noël
Makes 1 yule log

6 tablespoons unsweetened cocoa
  powder, divided
4 large eggs, separated
½ cup sugar, divided
1 tablespoon water
1 teaspoon vanilla extract
½ cup all-purpose flour
½ teaspoon cream of tartar
White Chocolate Buttercream
  (recipe follows)
Garnish: peppermint crunch morsels
  and fresh mint sprigs

1. Preheat oven to 375°. Spray bottom and sides of a 15x10-inch jelly-roll pan with nonstick cooking spray. Line baking pan with wax paper; spray with cooking spray, and sift 1 tablespoon cocoa powder over prepared paper.

2. In a large bowl, beat egg yolks at high speed with a mixer until thick and pale. Gradually beat in ¼ cup sugar. Add water and vanilla, beating until combined. Stir in flour and 3 tablespoons cocoa powder.

3. In a separate large bowl, beat egg whites and cream of tartar at high speed with a mixer until foamy. Gradually beat in remaining ¼ cup sugar, 1 tablespoon at a time, until stiff peaks form and sugar dissolves. Gently fold egg whites into chocolate mixture.

4. Spread batter evenly into prepared jelly-roll pan. Bake for 12 minutes. Sift 1 tablespoon cocoa powder in 15x10-inch rectangle on a clean kitchen towel. Using a knife, loosen sides of cake from pan. Immediately invert cake onto prepared towel. Peel off wax paper. Sift remaining 1 tablespoon cocoa powder over hot cake. Roll up cake and towel together, starting at narrow end. Cool completely.

5. Unroll cake, and remove towel. Spread cake with 1 cup White Chocolate Buttercream containing peppermint crunch morsels; carefully reroll cake. Cover and chill. Cut a 2-inch-thick diagonal slice from one end of cake roll.

6. Place cake roll, seam side down, onto a serving platter. Place cut piece of cake against side of roll at an angle to resemble tree knot. Spread remaining White Chocolate Buttercream evenly over cake. Garnish with peppermint crunch baking morsels and mint sprigs, if desired.

White Chocolate Buttercream
Makes 3 cups

1 cup butter, softened
3 tablespoons white chocolate
  liqueur
3 tablespoons milk
6 cups confectioners' sugar
½ cup peppermint crunch
  morsels

1. In a large bowl, beat butter at medium speed with a mixer until creamy. Beat in liqueur and milk. Gradually add confectioners' sugar, beating until smooth.

2. In a small bowl, place 1 cup White Chocolate Buttercream; stir in peppermint crunch morsels. Reserve remaining 2 cups buttercream to frost cake.

Orange Fig Scones
Makes 12 scones

2 cups all-purpose flour
¼ cup plus 2 tablespoons sugar, divided
1½ teaspoons baking powder
½ teaspoon salt
6 tablespoons butter
⅔ cup chopped dried figs
2 tablespoons orange zest
2 large eggs, divided
½ cup heavy cream
1 teaspoon vanilla extract
Garnish: whipped cream, orange zest twist, and nutmeg

1. Preheat oven to 400°. Line 2 baking sheets with parchment paper.

2. In a large bowl, combine flour, ¼ cup sugar, baking powder, and salt. Using a pastry blender, cut in butter until mixture is crumbly. Add figs and orange zest; mix well.

3. In a separate bowl, whisk together 1 egg, heavy cream, and vanilla. Add to flour mixture, and stir just until dough is combined (dough will be sticky).

4. Divide dough into 2 disks. On a lightly floured surface, roll half of dough into a 6x½-inch circle; cut into 6 wedges. Place on prepared baking sheet. Repeat with remaining dough.

5. In a small bowl, lightly beat remaining egg. Brush scones with beaten egg, and sprinkle with remaining 2 tablespoons sugar. Bake for 12 to 14 minutes or until lightly browned. Garnish with whipped cream, nutmeg, and orange zest twist, if desired.

Lemon Almond Pound Cake
Makes 1 pound cake

3 cups sifted all-purpose flour
¼ teaspoon baking soda
3 cups sugar
1 cup butter, softened
1½ tablespoons lemon zest
2 teaspoons lemon extract
6 large eggs, separated
1 cup sour cream
1 cup finely chopped slivered almonds
½ teaspoon salt
Lemon Glaze (recipe follows)
Garnish: sliced almonds

1. Preheat oven to 350°. Spray a 12-cup Bundt pan with nonstick baking spray with flour.

2. In a medium bowl, sift together flour and baking soda 3 times.

3. In a separate bowl, beat sugar and butter at medium speed with a mixer until fluffy. Add lemon zest and extract, beating to mix well. Add egg yolks, one at a time, beating well after each addition. Add flour mixture to butter mixture alternately with sour cream, beginning and ending with flour mixture. Stir in almonds.

4. In a medium bowl, beat egg whites and salt at high speed with a mixer until stiff peaks form. Fold egg white mixture into batter until well combined.

5. Spoon batter into prepared pan. Bake for 1 hour to 1 hour and 10 minutes or until a wooden pick inserted in center comes out clean. Cool in pan for 10 minutes on a wire rack.

6. Invert cake onto wire rack, and brush with Lemon Glaze. Garnish with sliced almonds, if desired.

Lemon Glaze
Makes about 1 cup

1 cup light corn syrup
⅓ cup lemon juice
¼ cup sugar
1 tablespoon lemon zest

1. In a medium saucepan over medium heat, combine corn syrup, lemon juice, sugar, and lemon zest.

2. Bring to a simmer, stirring frequently, until mixture thickens, about 4 to 5 minutes. Remove from heat, and cool slightly.

ORANGE FIG SCONES

LEMON ALMOND
POUND CAKE

Gingerbread Scones
Makes 12 scones

2 cups self-rising flour
¼ cup firmly packed dark brown
   sugar
1½ teaspoons ground ginger
1 teaspoon ground cinnamon
⅛ teaspoon ground cloves
½ cup cold unsalted butter,
   cut into cubes
⅓ cup buttermilk
⅓ cup unsulfured molasses
1 large egg, lightly beaten
2 pieces crystallized ginger, cut into
   ⅛-inch squares
1 cup cold heavy cream
3 tablespoons confectioners' sugar

1. Preheat oven to 400°. Line a baking sheet with parchment paper; set aside.

2. In a large bowl, whisk together flour, brown sugar, ginger, cinnamon, and cloves. Using a pastry blender, cut butter into flour mixture until mixture is crumbly.

3. In a medium bowl, whisk together buttermilk and molasses. Add buttermilk mixture to flour mixture, and stir just until dough is combined (dough will be sticky).

4. On a lightly floured surface pat dough into a ½-inch-thick circle; using a small gingerbread man-shaped cutter, cut out 12 scones, rerolling scraps as necessary.

5. Place scones on prepared baking sheet. Using a pastry brush, brush tops of scones with beaten egg, and place 2 squares of crystallized ginger on center of body to make buttons. Bake for 8 minutes or until golden brown. Cool on pans for 3 minutes. Remove from pans, and cool completely on a wire rack.

6. In a large bowl, beat cream and confectioners' sugar at medium-high speed with a mixer until soft peaks form. Serve whipped cream with scones.

CHAI LATTE

CANDY CANE
COCOA COFFEE

Chai Latte
Makes 12 to 14 servings

8 cups water
4 cups whole milk
¾ cup sugar
3 orange slices
2 cinnamon sticks
1 tablespoon whole cloves
1 whole nutmeg, grated
¾ teaspoon whole black
    peppercorns
6 black tea bags
Garnish: cinnamon sticks

1. In a large Dutch oven, combine water, milk, sugar, orange slices, cinnamon sticks, cloves, nutmeg, peppercorns, and tea bags. Bring to a boil over medium-high heat, and cook, stirring occasionally, until sugar dissolves. Remove from heat; let stand 15 minutes. Strain mixture, and discard solids. Garnish with cinnamon sticks, if desired. Serve immediately.

Candy Cane Cocoa Coffee
Makes 12 to 14 servings

1½ cups unsweetened cocoa
    powder
1½ cups sugar
6 cups hot strong coffee
9 cups whole milk
1½ teaspoons peppermint extract
Garnish: peppermint sticks

1. In a large Dutch oven, combine cocoa powder and sugar. Gradually whisk in coffee and milk, and cook over medium-high heat until tiny bubbles form around the edge of the pan. Remove from heat; stir in extract. Garnish with peppermint sticks, if desired. Serve immediately.

Spirited Eggnog Coffee Punch
Makes 6 to 8 servings

4 cups eggnog
3 cups hot strong coffee
1 cup bourbon
3 tablespoons cinnamon syrup*
Garnish: whipped cream and
    ground cinnamon

1. In a large saucepan, heat eggnog and coffee over medium heat until hot. Stir in bourbon and cinnamon syrup. Top each serving with whipped cream, and sprinkle with cinnamon, if desired. Serve immediately.

*We used Monin Cinnamon Premium Gourmet Syrup, available at monin.com.

Orange Hot Chocolate
Makes 6 to 8 servings

½ cup sugar
1 cup unsweetened cocoa
   powder
4 cups heavy whipping cream
4 cups whole milk
8 ounces dark chocolate, chopped
1 cup orange liqueur
Garnish: mini marshmallows

1. In a large saucepan over medium heat, combine sugar and cocoa powder. Gradually whisk in cream and milk until smooth. Cook, whisking constantly, until tiny bubbles form around the edge of the pan. Add chocolate, stirring until melted. Remove from heat; stir in liqueur. Serve each with mini marshmallows, if desired. Serve immediately.

Butterscotch Cider
Makes 12 to 14 servings

12 cups apple cider
3 tablespoons chopped fresh
   ginger
1½ teaspoons whole allspice
1½ teaspoons whole cloves
1 whole nutmeg, grated
2 cinnamon sticks
1½ cups butterscotch Schnapps
   liqueur
Garnish: apple slices

1. In a large Dutch oven, add cider, ginger, allspice, cloves, nutmeg, and cinnamon sticks; bring to a boil over medium-high heat. Remove from heat; stir in liqueur. Let stand for 10 minutes. Strain, discarding solids. Top with apples slices, if desired. Serve immediately.

Creamy Cranberry-White Chocolate Delight

Makes 6 to 8 servings

3 (4-ounce) bars white chocolate, chopped
2 cups heavy whipping cream, divided
3 cups whole milk
3 cups cranberry juice
Garnish: fresh cranberries and white chocolate curls

1. In a large saucepan over medium heat, add chocolate; gradually whisk in 1½ cups cream, whisking constantly, until chocolate is melted. Whisk in milk and cranberry juice; cook until heated through. Whisk in remaining ½ cup cream. Garnish with skewered cranberries, and top with white chocolate curls, if desired. Serve immediately.

Collecting for the KITCHEN

The holidays are a season of remembrance. Nostalgic symbols of Christmases past pull at our heartstrings, giving us the desire to decorate with timeless treasures such as baking tools, delicate glassware, and even festive tin molds.

Timeless Treasures

CHOCOLATE MOLDS HAVE
DELIGHTED PEOPLE OF ALL AGES
FOR ALMOST TWO CENTURIES. THEY
CONTINUE TO EVOLVE IN THE MANY
WAYS THEY ARE USED TODAY.

Chocolate molds add a festive and unique touch to a tabletop Christmas tree. Since both have ties to Germany, they offer a nice pairing and a nod to their heritage. The variety of molds will make your tree worthy of a closer look.

Although chocolate molds were first created almost 200 years ago, they're as popular today as they've ever been. These delicately designed treasures were originally made to delight children, but it seems that it's the adults who have become the devoted collectors. Many people remember these fun shapes and the wonderful chocolate statues from their childhood and want to share these special memories with their own children and grandchildren. Thankfully, these sturdy little soldiers have withstood the test of time and can be passed from generation to generation without many signs of aging.

One reason that people of all ages enjoy chocolate molds is because of their versatility. Of course, they will always be best known for making decadent chocolate treats, but over the years it has been found that they have more than one talent. Molds can be used to make unique butter pats to liven up your holiday table, as well as adding a bit of old-world charm when decorating your tree. They can be used in Christmas craft projects and may also be used to make wonderful holiday gifts of soaps and candles—these can even be scented like chocolate to remind everyone of their original purpose!

However you decide to use these timeless treasures, you can be sure they will continue to delight for centuries to come.

A Serious Santa

By the 1920s, chocolate molds were so popular that there were more than 50,000 designs. Some collectors limit their search to one specific subject, such as Santa. This German Santa by Heris circa 1920 is unusual in his stern appearance and the presence of the much-dreaded "switches."

Glass Beauties

CHRISTMAS IS THE TIME OF YEAR THAT EVERYONE
ENJOYS ENTERTAINING FAMILY AND FRIENDS
AND SHARING SPECIAL MEALS TOGETHER.

Antique cake stands in
holiday colors are perfect
for showcasing these festive
sugar cookies and ginger-
bread cutouts. Elevating
your decorated treats adds
pizzazz to your holiday table.

Shining Stars
Mixing the size, shape, and
color of cake stands creates
an eye-catching display. Even
non-homemade cookies and
treats look blissfully delicious
when presented beautifully.

Let your holiday table be a focal point for showing your individual style of decorating, as well as your culinary skills. An elegant way to spice up a selection of desserts is to use a variety of vintage or antique cake stands to showcase your treats. Although these sparkling beauties were originally made in the late 1800s exclusively for cake, they can be used today to display cookies, candies, and other desserts with effortless style. Cake stands were made in several sizes, shapes, heights, and colors, so they lend themselves easily to displaying beautiful holiday fare. The Victorians were fond of stacking cake stands with treats several levels high to fascinate their guests. The diminutive children's cake stands were originally made for teaching children how to entertain, but now are the perfect size for candies and mints. An array of red and green stands filled with your creations makes a dazzling centerpiece for any holiday meal or party. Whether large or small, round or square, clear or colored, cake stands always brighten up your table and delight your guests.

A Vintage Touch

SPICING UP YOUR KITCHEN WITH VINTAGE
RED AND GREEN BAKING ITEMS WILL ADD A
FESTIVE FEEL TO ANY HOLIDAY GATHERING.

Many Christmas memories revolve around our kitchens and the times we've spent there with loved ones, baking our favorite treats. Although we decorate our homes from the tip of the chimney to the mailbox, we often bypass the room in which we spend most of our time. Spicing up our kitchens with vintage bakeware will give them a charming splash of holiday color. It's a wonderful time of year to bring out Mother's red-handled rolling pin or Grandma's butter churn. You can even include some newer bits and pieces that have an antique look. Mixing the ages and styles of items will give your kitchen its own personal touch. Reconnecting with these cherished odds and ends will not only make your kitchen look holiday-special but will enhance the time and memories that are shared there.

This Dazey jar butter churn from grandmother's farm is a great place to display your Christmas ornaments. It looks cheerful on this flea market-find vintage bar stool.

Finding old cookie cutters at a consignment shop or antiques store will add to your collection for just a few dollars. There are so many fun shapes and sizes to make a variety of cookies for your holiday guests. Your little cowboys will love this friendly fellow with the holsters on his hips!

Splendid Storage

These vintage rolling pins from the '30s and '40s store beautifully in this timeworn wooden bucket originally made for mincemeat. You can select your choice of size or color at your fingertips when rolling out cookies and pies. Children will love to choose their favorite while learning to bake.

Resources

FRONT COVER
Christmas coffee cups and saucers from lenox.com; cake stand from edgarsbakery.com

PAGE 4
Ornaments and gold metal garland from codyfosterandco.com

PAGE 8-9
Gold painted wooden place mat and cranberry red crystal from clarkantiquesgallery.com

PAGE 16-23
Pitcher, glasses, and wicker chargers from williams-sonoma.com; plaid tablecloth and napkins from frenchlaundryhome.com; christmas trees and silver deer from codyfosterandco.com; Christmas tree plate from fiestafactorydirect.com; small sauce pitcher from williams-sonoma.com; casserole dishes from skyrosdesigns.com; red cake stand and silver tray with handles from harmonylanding.com

PAGE 28-37
Wooden candlesticks, white ironstone pitcher, glass ornaments, antique wire breadbasket, and black and white transferware vegetable bowl from mulberryheightsantiques.com; white ironstone soup tureen from Village Firefly Inc.,

205-870-4560; pewter cake stand and pewter charger from brombergs.com

PAGE 44-47
Large round silver tray and red and white transferware from Tricia's Treasures, triciastreasures.com; black and white transferware and white ironstone vegetable bowl from mulberryheightsantiques.com

PAGE 52-61
Silver trays, silver beverage chiller, gold-painted wooden chargers, and cranberry red crystal from clarkantiquesgallery.com

PAGE 73-78
Vintage ornaments from christopherradko.com; Revol bakeware from surlatable.com; Cutlery caddy from downmulberrylane.com

PAGE 87
Serving tray from wendellaugust.com

PAGE 106
Stockings from frenchlaundryhome.com; white deer from codyfosterandco.com

PAGE 122
Holiday wreath pillow from potterybarn.com

PAGE 136
Selected items from seibelscatalog.com

PAGE 162-179
Gift tags by Cavallini from paper-source.com

PAGE 183
Glass jar and glass container from worldmarket.com

PAGE 186
Napkins from williams-sonoma.com

PAGE 190
Herbs from bonnieplants.com

PAGE 201
Cake stand from edgarsbakery.com

PAGE 222
Antique chocolate molds from Wendy Mullen, victorianchocolatemolds.com

PAGE 226
Cake Stands from T.L.C. Antiques, 719-641-8566 or tlcantiques@earthlink.net

PAGE 230-235
Vintage kitchen and baking tools from Consignment of Collectables, 719-528-5922

Recipe Index

CHOCOLATE
Almond Cookie Truffles 170
Bittersweet Chocolate Sauce 205
Bittersweet Mocha Torte 205
Brandy Cream in Chocolate Cups 93
Chocolate Cake Roll with Fig Filling and
    Kumquat-Pineapple Syrup 49
Chocolate Ganache Icing 84
Chocolate Hazelnut Cookie Truffles 170
Chocolate Mousse 205
Chocolate Mousse Pie 36
Chocolate Pound Cake with Mint Icing 61
Chocolate Toffee Trifle 36
Creamy Cranberry-White Chocolate
    Delight 219
Dark Chocolate Raspberry Mousse Cake 84
Frozen German Chocolate Pie 70
Kahlúa and Coffee Fudge 98
Meringue Surprises 184
Spiced Chocolate Truffles 188
White Chocolate Buttercream 210
White Chocolate Mousse Cake 43

COCONUT
Coconut Tarts 176
Frozen German Chocolate Pie 70
Hello Dolly Bars 184
Pineapple-Coconut Mini Loaves 174

COOKIES, BARS, AND SQUARES
Almond Cookie Truffles 170
Chocolate Hazelnut Cookie Truffles 170
Gumdrop Cookie Bites 164
Gingerbread Men 176
Hello Dolly Bars 184
Homemade Granola Bars 170
Karen's Cocoons 184
Lemon Squares 181
Meringue Surprises 184
Oatmeal Cookies 185
Raspberry Swirl Cheesecake Bars 173

CRANBERRIES
Caramel-glazed Cranberry Bundt Cake 23
Cranberry Apple Tea 56
Cranberries and Brie Wrapped in Phyllo 105
Cranberry Cheddar Wafers 172
Cranberry-Cider Fizz 23
Cranberry-Orange Chutney 67
Cranberry-Raspberry Liqueur 178
Cranberry Splash 27
Creamy Cranberry-White Chocolate
    Delight 219
Orange-Cranberry Filling 209
Wild Rice with Cranberries 4/

DESSERTS *(see also Cakes; Cookies, Bars, and Squares; Pies and Tarts)*
Brandy Cream in Chocolate Cups 93
Bread Pudding with Praline Sauce 78
Chocolate Toffee Trifle 36
Creamy Mixed Berries 61
Gingerbread Fingers with Orange Crème
    Filling 83

DRESSINGS AND STUFFINGS
Cornbread Dressing 42
Roasted Turkey with Sausage Stuffing 64

EGGS
Parmesan-baked Eggs with Toast Points 20

FILLINGS
Chocolate Mousse 205
Fig Filling 49
Orange-Cranberry Filling 209
Orange Crème Filling 83
Raspberry Mousse 84
Sweet Potato Filling 50

FISH *(see Seafood)*

FROSTINGS
Black Walnut Icing 206
Chocolate Ganache Icing 84
Cream Cheese Frosting 181
Fluffy White Frosting 200
Mint Icing 61
Molasses Frosting 50
Orange-Cream Cheese Frosting 209
White Chocolate Buttercream 210

FRUIT *(see also Apples, Pineapple, Raspberries, Strawberries)*
Creamy Mixed Berries 61
Hot Curried Fruit 27
Sugared Fruit and Rosemary 200

GLAZES
Caramel Glaze 23
Lemon Glaze 211
Orange Glaze 43

GRITS
Double Cheese Grits Casserole 27

HAM
Ham and Jarlsberg Sandwiches 82
Ham Steaks with Maple and Mustard 19
Prosciutto and Brie Dip 97
Spinach, Prosciutto, and Roasted Red
    Pepper Quiche 56

LEMON
Lemon Almond Pound Cake 211
Lemon Glaze 211
Lemon-Glazed Miniature Cakes 91
Lemon-Honey Vinaigrette 30
Lemon Squares 181
Lemon-Thyme Green Beans and
    Fingerling Potatoes 67

ONIONS
Brussels Sprouts with Bacon and
    Pearl Onions 30
Caramelized Onions 83

ORANGES
Cranberry-Orange Chutney 67
Easy Orange Rolls 42
Orange-Cranberry Filling 209
Orange-Cream Cheese Frosting 209
Orange Crème Filling 83
Orange Curd 164
Orange Fig Scones 211
Orange Glaze 43
Orange Hot Chocolate 218
Orange, Olive, and Watercress Salad 55

PEPPERS
Holiday Italian Salad 40
Spinach, Prosciutto, and Roasted Red
    Pepper Quiche 56

PIES AND TARTS
Chocolate Mousse Pie 36
Coconut Tarts 176
Frozen German Chocolate Pie 70
Pecan Pie Tartlets 101
Spiced Jam Tartlets 188
Spinach, Prosciutto, and Roasted Red
    Pepper Quiche 56
Tangerine Pie 70

PINEAPPLE
Kumquat-Pineapple Syrup 49
Pineapple-Coconut Mini Loaves 174

PORK
Apple-glazed Crown Pork Roast 46
Pork and Sausage Cassoulet 33

POTATOES
Broccoli and Cheese Stuffed Potatoes 42
Lemon-Thyme Green Beans and
    Fingerling Potatoes 67
Mini Potato Skins with Horseradish
    Dipping Sauce 97
Potato Casserole with Smoked Salmon
    and Horseradish Cream 21

PUMPKIN
Butternut Squash, Pumpkin, and
    Apple Soup 64

RASPBERRIES
Cranberry-Raspberry Liqueur 178
Dark Chocolate Raspberry Mousse Cake 84
Raspberry Swirl Cheesecake Bars 173

RICE
Parsley Rice 75
Wild Rice with Cranberries 47

SALAD DRESSINGS AND VINAIGRETTES
Creamy Balsamic Italian Dressing 40
Lemon-Honey Vinaigrette 30
Sun-dried Tomato Vinaigrette 167

SALADS
Holiday Italian Salad 40
Orange, Olive, and Watercress Salad 55
Seasonal Spinach Salad 30
Strawberry-Kiwifruit Salad 21
Warm Baby Spinach, Bacon, and
    Green Bean Salad 46

SANDWICHES
Ham and Jarlsberg Sandwiches 82
Roast Beef Finger Sandwiches with
    Kalamata Mustard Butter 91
Roast Beef Roll-ups with Maytag Blue
    Cheese and Caramelized Onions 82

SAUCES
Bittersweet Chocolate Sauce 205
Creole Mustard Sauce 77
Horseradish Dipping Sauce 97
Marinara Sauce 100
Orange Curd 164
Praline Sauce 78
Saffron Aïoli 91
Strawberry Sauce 43

SAUSAGE
Pork and Sausage Cassoulet 33
Roasted Turkey with Sausage Stuffing 64
Sausage Breakfast Casserole 27
Sausage Wontons 105
Shrimp and Andouille Gumbo 75

SEAFOOD
Potato Casserole with Smoked Salmon
    and Horseradish Cream 21
Shrimp and Andouille Gumbo 75
Shrimp Mousse with Saffron Aïoli
    in Phyllo Cups 91

SOUPS AND STEWS
Butternut Squash, Pumpkin, and
    Apple Soup 64
Creamy Apple Soup 55
Creamy Herbed Spinach Soup 82
Shrimp and Andouille Gumbo 75

SPINACH
Creamy Herbed Spinach Soup 82
Seasonal Spinach Salad 30
Spinach, Prosciutto, and Roasted Red
    Pepper Quiche 56
Warm Baby Spinach, Bacon, and
    Green Bean Salad 46

SQUASH
Butternut Squash, Pumpkin, and
    Apple Soup 64
Squash and Zucchini Casserole 40
Zucchini with Limas and Tomatoes 76

STRAWBERRIES
Strawberry-Kiwifruit Salad 21
Strawberry Sauce 43

SWEET POTATOES
Sweet Potato Filling 50
Sweet Potato Layer Cake with
    Molasses Frosting 50
Sweet Potato-Pecan Muffins 25

TOMATOES
Sun-dried Tomato Vinaigrette 167
Zucchini with Limas and Tomatoes 76

TOPPINGS
Apricot Preserves 92
Cranberry-Orange Chutney 67
Herb Butter 34
Horseradish Cream 21
Kumquat-Pineapple Syrup 49
Pecan Topping 50
Sugared Fruit and Rosemary 200
Walnut-Spice Butter 19

TURKEY
Deep-fried Turkey 41
Roasted Turkey with Sausage Stuffing 64

VEGETABLES AND SIDE DISHES
Broccoli and Cheese Stuffed Potatoes 42
Brussels Sprouts with Bacon and
    Pearl Onions 30
Double Cheese Grits Casserole 27
Glazed Carrots 40
Lemon-Thyme Green Beans and
    Fingerling Potatoes 67
Parsley Rice 75
Roasted Root Vegetables with Rosemary 35
Rustic Macaroni and Cheese 75
Squash and Zucchini Casserole 40
Whipped Cauliflower 76
Wild Rice with Cranberries 47
Zucchini with Limas and Tomatoes 76

ZUCCHINI
Squash and Zucchini Casserole 40
Zucchini with Limas and Tomatoes 76